THE HOMEOWNER'S HANDBOOK OF POWER TOOLS

THE HOMEOWNER'S HANDBOOK OF POWER TOOLS

Len Buckwalter

FUNK & WAGNALLS

New York

For a listing of the companies and organizations that have generously provided illustrations for reproduction in this book, see page 225.

Designed by S. S. Drate

Manufactured in the United States of America

Library of Congress Cataloging in Publication Data
Buckwalter, Len.
  The homeowner's handbook of power tools.
  Includes index.
  1. Power tools. I. Title.
TT153.5.B82   621.9   75-28061
ISBN 0-308-10226-6
10 9 8 7 6 5 4 3 2 1

CONTENTS

1

INTRODUCTION   *1*

2

DRILL   *16*

3

SABER SAW   *34*

4

CIRCULAR SAW   *50*

5

SANDER   *65*

148349

6

SOLDERING IRON AND PROPANE TORCH 78

7

BENCH GRINDER AND HAND-HELD GRINDER 94

8

ROUTER 109

9

RADIAL ARM SAW 122

10

LATHE 135

11

TABLE SAW 148

12

SCROLL (JIG) SAW 163

13

BAND SAW 172

14

CHAIN SAW 181

15

HEDGE TRIMMER   194

16

ROTARY LAWN MOWER   202

17

BUY OR RENT?   212

APPENDIX   225

INDEX   227

THE
HOMEOWNER'S
HANDBOOK
OF
POWER TOOLS

1

INTRODUCTION

I moved into my first house a month after an expert warned me not to buy it. He'd spent a lifetime in the building business, and he merely walked through the 800-square-foot ranch house and jabbed a few beams in the basement. When we were outside, he spat on the driveway and delivered the appraisal.

"Not a penny over seventeen."

His reasons were sound. The house was small, located in a stable neighborhood that showed little sign of a real estate boom—and the owner stood firm at $20,000. I bought the place anyway. What Henry (my expert) didn't know and couldn't predict was that my questionable investment would someday declare a dividend of 235 percent. My secret? A homeowner's greatest asset after his mortgage banker—the power tool.

Soon after I moved in, I inherited my first important power tool—free— from a generous brother. It was old, so old that replacement blades were impossible to obtain. The tool was a portable circular saw of awesome twisting force. When I first pressed its snarling teeth into a two-by-four it was clear why carpenters boast they can build a house with a circular saw. In the next ten years I would turn, with the help of this formidable machine, a tiny dwelling into a spacious home of twice the area.

A dank basement became a wood-paneled playroom. Heavy timbers fell under the blade to fill a void between house and garage with an unusual glass-walled dining room. The kitchen was gutted of greasy cupboards and modernized. The garage became an elegant bedroom suite and bath.

These improvements were done before the roaring inflation of the mid-seventies, but the economics were impressive by any standards. The original 800-square-foot house, bloated by inflation, would have sold for approximately $33,000. With improvements and expansion it went for $47,000. Out of the profit came the cost of materials—about $2,000—and my eager labor.

These figures pale before the value returned by the power tools. Including that free circular saw, kept alive by a local sharpener, the cost of the power tools equaled little more than $100! That included every basic item for home remodeling—drill, saber saw, circular saw, and sander. With these tools I could cut framing lumber, saw building materials to size, trim paneling, and prepare surfaces for finishing.

With a tidy profit in my pocket, it was time to go househunting again. Henry had retired so I decided, after ten years of weekend home construction, to do my own appraisal. I even felt knowledgeable about signs of termites—a pile of tiny wings on the basement floor and mud tunnels on the foundation—but the real estate agents cracked my confidence. What they billed as the "handyman special" turned out to be a collection of sagging, shored-up shacks beyond redemption. Isn't it true, anyway, that a man who does his own house evaluation has a fool for an appraiser? I summoned an expert.

He was no Henry. A building contractor, the man scrutinized my prospective house, a tired-looking but sturdy structure, like a professor of architecture. He recorded each observation on a clipboard and uttered scholarly comments that ran the gamut from inadequate attic vents to foundation cracks. After he carefully weighed his findings I asked if the house was worth the asking price.

"That's something only you can decide."

I saw my $35 appraisal fee fly out the window, a casualty of "expert's syndrome": the greater the expertise, the less decisive the judgment. Henry, at least, had delivered a definite answer.

"What would it cost to bring this house into first-class condition?" I asked.

He looked at his board and toted up seven items. "Five thousand dollars . . . at least. I may have to tear out a wall behind the bathtub. Looks wet."

Perceiving a conflict of interest between appraiser and repairer, I thanked the man and elected to invest $300 in more power tools. With sophisticated instruments to improve my speed and accuracy, I'd attempt to fix the house myself.

The first wall came tumbling down a few weeks after I moved in. I planned to transform a grim kitchen into a bright dining area. The expensive repairs suggested by the inspector-builder proved to be piddling compared with

A major home improvement is speeded by power tools. Author's antique, but adequate, circular saw is on table at left.

the house's real needs, and I now estimated the worth of my power tools at $183 an ounce—pure gold. The value of the house soared as it acquired the custom touches that send buyers into ecstasy and professional carpenters into a frenzy.

But working with power tools is more than a money-saving tactic. The acute shortage of skilled tradesmen that began in the early fifties shows no sign of abating. With increasing opportunities for jobs in offices and factories, fewer young people are willing to risk the uncertain, arduous life of a carpenter or plumber. *Time* magazine gave a wry report on the problem: when people in Spokane, Washington, called a local plumber, a telephone recording device replied: "If you have a plumbing problem, please write down the nature of your problem and mail it to me. If this is an emergency, write 'Rush' on the letter. All letters will be judged on the basis of neatness and originality."

In the fifties the power tool industry began to respond to this situation. Before that time, an amateur shopping for a motorized tool at a local store would find little more than a $\frac{1}{4}$-inch electric drill. Powerful saws and other such commercial products were bought by carpenters in lumber and building-supply outlets that catered to the trade. But as the public's appetite for power tools grew, the industry "consumerized" itself. Professional-type products started to appear on the shelves of neighborhood retail outlets and found their way into the catalogues of giant mail-order houses. Tools with husky motors of 2 and 3 horsepower, expensive ball bearings, and ponderous metal housings were scaled down to the lower price and durability requirements of the home hobbyist. Instead of packaging their wares according to commercial buying practices, where a motor and accessories are sold separately, the industry began to offer tools that were "ready to run."

A burgeoning do-it-yourself movement that appeared in the late fifties clinched the trend. Tired of cookie-cutter products, shoddy workmanship, or a daily job that held neither delight nor surprise, more people felt impelled to create their own practical and esthetic objects. The ranks of do-it-yourselfers swelled mightily in the seventies as the costs of maintaining a home and possessions reached alarming levels. As doing it yourself has become a matter of survival, power tools have become the secret of successful survival. This trend was lugubriously summed up by an advertising executive at a hardware convention in 1974: "Business is terrible. The manufacturers are selling all the power tools they can make. They don't need to advertise!"

But there was another side to the power tool boom. Concern about consumer product safety, which started with the automobile, began to spread to

Safety glasses or goggles protect the eyes against flying chips and other debris.

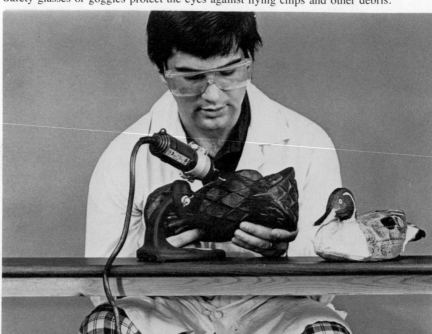

SAFETY RULES

1. *Ground All Tools—Unless Double-Insulated.* If tool is equipped with three-prong plug, it should be plugged into a three-hole electrical receptacle. If adapter is used to accommodate two-prong receptacle, the adapter wire must be attached to a known ground. Never remove third prong.
2. *Keep Guards in Place* and in working order.
3. *Keep Work Area Clean.* Cluttered areas and benches invite accidents.
4. *Avoid Dangerous Environment.* Don't use power tools in damp or wet locations. Keep work area well lit.
5. *Keep Children Away.* All visitors should be kept safe distance from work area.
6. *Don't Force Tool.* It will do the job better and safer at the rate for which it was designed.
7. *When Leaving the Work Area* temporarily, tools should be stored out of reach of children.
8. *Wear Proper Apparel.* No loose clothing or jewelry to get caught in moving parts. Rubber gloves and footwear are recommended when working outdoors.
9. *Use Safety Glasses.* Should be worn with most tools. Also face or dust mask if cutting operation is dusty.
10. *Don't Abuse Cord.* Never carry tool by cord or yank it to disconnect from receptacle. Keep cord from heat, oil, and sharp edges.
11. *Secure Work.* Use clamps or a vise to hold work. It's safer than using your hand and it frees both hands to operate tool.
12. *Don't Overreach.* Keep proper footing and balance at all times.
13. *Disconnect Tools.* Disconnect when not in use; before servicing; when changing accessories such as blades, bits, cutters, etc.
14. *Remove Adjusting Keys and Wrenches.* Form habit of checking to see that keys and adjusting wrenches are removed from tool before turning it on.
15. *Avoid Accidental Starting.* Don't carry plugged-in tool with finger on switch.
16. *Know Your Power Tool.* Learn its applications and limitations as well as the specific potential hazards peculiar to this tool.

power tools. There were frightening reports of lethal lawn mowers, shock hazard in electrical products, and injury from unguarded blades and spinning machinery. To stave off the threat of federal regulation, the industry sponsored the Power Tool Institute (PTI), to codify and promote safe operating rules. Although these rules contain no surprises for the cautious worker, they will, if faithfully followed, reduce risk in power tool operation to nearly zero.

But rules alone are not enough. Superbly trained rule-abiders—from airline pilots to diamond cutters—are occasionally victims of accidents. To reduce the hazard present from skimpy design, more power tools are being routinely fitted with protective features that were once "extras" on deluxe models. Let's consider several examples.

One of the earliest techniques to reduce electrical shock was the *3-wire cord*. In a conventional cord, 2 wires carry current inside the tool housing. If the insulation jacket covering the wires breaks, a live wire could contact the housing and make it electrically "hot." You may not be aware of the breakdown until you hold the tool and simultaneously touch a metal object connected to an electrical ground. It may be a sink faucet, heating duct, or some other mass of metal in the home. When the circuit is complete—from damaged wire to tool case, through your hand and body to ground—you'll be shocked. It takes only $^5/_{1000}$ ampere to deliver a dangerous jolt. To make matters worse, a power tool is often operated in conditions that favor the hazard. Mechanical vibration may break down the insulation, or you may grip the tool with damp hands—two factors which improve the contact. You may be standing on a basement floor or working outdoors on bare earth. Both surfaces are excellent electrical grounds.

MAINTENANCE CHECK LIST

1. *Cord Sets and Extension Cords.* Visually check cords for cuts or other previous damage. Examine plugs for damage to the ground terminal. If the ground terminal is missing, the plug should be replaced.
2. *Switch.* Check mechanical operation of the switch with the plug disconnected; it should be free of excessive drag and binding. Also check for insecure mounting and for any other obvious defects.
3. *Chucks, Collets, and Other Tool-Holding Devices.* Check that parts are in good functional condition. Also check that proper-size wrenches and keys are available.
4. *Guards.* Check guards for proper installation. Movable guards should function smoothly.
5. *Housings and General Hardware.* Check general condition of housings for defects or damage. Replace missing hardware and tighten all loose bolts and fittings.
6. *Adjustments.* Make any necessary adjustments following manufacturer's recommendations.
7. *Blades and Bits.* Check for any damage or defects. Resharpen as required and reinstall in accordance with manufacturer's recommendations. Use only those attachments recommended by the manufacturer.
8. *Mechanical Operation.* If possible, the tool should be rotated by hand to assure that all parts operate freely and no internal damage to the drive train or bearings has occurred.
9. *Current Leakage Test.* This test should be performed using an approved ground fault interrupter (GFI), with the tool in each of its modes of operation (forward, reverse, etc.). The tool should also be operated at no load to check commutation. Any tool that trips the GFI should be taken out of service, identified with a red tag as unsafe, and repaired in accordance with the manufacturer's recommendations.

The Power Tool Institute suggests that small children be kept well clear of tools.

Place good support under work and use clamps, if possible, as at lower right.

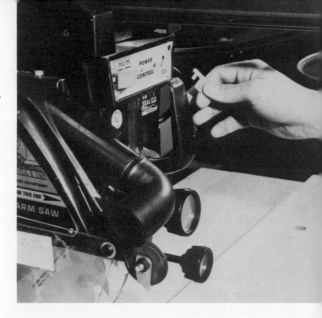

A key interlock prevents accidental or unauthorized starting of power tool.

A 3-wire cord protects by detouring current away from your body. Besides the cord's two wires, a third conductor connects to the tool's metal case, while its other end goes to an electrical ground through a third prong on the power plug. If wiring insulation breaks down, the current finds an easier path to ground through the case rather than through your body.

A drawback is that 3-wire sockets are not installed in most houses—though many new homes have them because of changes in the National Electrical Code. To operate a 3-wire cord in a conventional 2-wire socket an adapter must ground the extra wire, usually through the screw which holds on the outlet's cover plate. This is not always practical because that screw may not be a ground. If you don't know whether a ground occurs at the cover plate, have an electrician check and, if necessary, convert it. Another bothersome feature of the 3-wire cord is that extension cords must also be 3-wire to maintain an uninterrupted ground between tool and wall outlet.

A recently devised and far more convenient system for protection against shock hazard is *double insulation*. As the name implies, the tool is insulated two ways: by a conventional insulation jacket on bare wires and by a *dielectric* housing, which is one that cannot conduct current. If the internal insulation breaks down, you are protected by a second electrical barrier. Double insulation can be easily spotted—the housing is mainly plastic instead of metal.

An important advantage of double insulation is that because of the tool's protective construction it needs neither a third wire nor grounding. Now you can plug into any type of outlet, or use common extension cords. You'll never have to resort to such dangerous tactics as breaking off a plug's third prong so it fits a two-slot outlet, or leaving the grounding pigtail on an adapter dangling free.

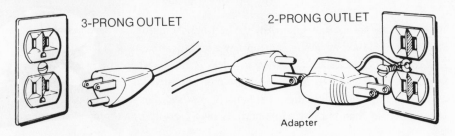

3-PRONG OUTLET   2-PRONG OUTLET

Adapter

Proper grounding with a 3-prong plug. Cord may plug directly into a 3-prong outlet (left); with a 2-prong outlet, an adapter must be used and a green pigtail wire installed under screwhead (right).

The boon of double insulation is partly offset by the plastic construction. Modern plastics are tough but they may not sustain the abuse that a metal-enclosed tool will. Another problem may occur in cleaning the plastic. The material could be damaged by chlorinated cleaning agents, carbon tetrachloride, or gasoline. Use only household detergents like Ajax, Mr. Clean, or Handy Andy on double-insulation housings.

Much of the time a portable power tool must be used with an extension cord because the short cable supplied by the manufacturer is inadequate for many jobs away from the bench. A standard extension cord about 10 feet in length with No. 18 conductors is sufficient for small portable tools. When the run is longer or the machine draws heavy amperage, choose a cord that's heavy enough to bear the load. Thin wires overheat and cause slow motor speed, internal heating, poor efficiency, and even permanent damage. Manufacturers often say a tool must be operated within 5 or 10 percent of the nameplate voltage, and choosing the right extension cord is one prerequisite.

To determine a safe extension cord, check the chart below for the desired length against the tool's operating amperage. Find the number of amperes, as

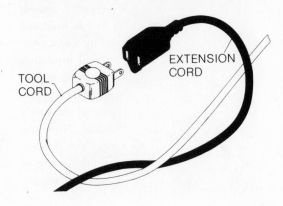

TOOL CORD

EXTENSION CORD

A simple knot prevents tool cord from being pulled out of extension socket.

shown on the tool's nameplate, in the left-hand column. Then determine the cord's length, looking along the top row (lengths are given for either 115 or 230 volts). The wire size, or gauge, to select is shown where the two figures intersect. If the exact size is not available pick the next-thicker wire. (Note that as wire becomes heavier, the wire gauge grows *smaller*. For example, No. 16 wire is thicker than No. 18 wire and thus may carry more current.)

Ampere Rating Range	Length of Cord (ft.)								
	115 V: 25	50	100	150	200	250	300	400	500
	230 V: 50	100	200	300	400	500	600	800	1000
0–2	18	18	18	16	16	14	14	12	12
2–3	18	18	16	14	14	12	12	10	10
3–4	18	18	16	14	12	12	10	10	8
4–5	18	18	14	12	12	10	10	8	8
5–6	18	16	14	12	10	10	8	8	6
6–8	18	16	12	10	10	8	6	6	6
8–10	18	14	12	10	8	8	6	6	4
10–12	16	14	10	8	8	6	6	4	4
12–14	16	12	10	8	6	6	6	4	2
14–16	16	12	10	8	6	6	4	4	2
16–18	14	12	8	8	6	4	4	2	2
18–20	14	12	8	6	6	4	4	2	2

One hazard with a power cord seems straight from the scenario of a *Bugs Bunny* cartoon, but it's a real danger. It is unwittingly cutting your cord in half while sawing along a line. This is solved by routing the cord well away from the guideline on the work. If you've purchased a new tool recently introduced on the market, be sure the designer considered the cord factor. A neighbor of mine purchased a radial arm saw that clamped its cable too close to the blade. One day he neatly sheared it off. After a blistering letter to the manufacturer, my friend, an industrial designer, received an apology. Future runs of the tool, it said, would have the cord on the opposite side of the saw.

Most power tools work well on an ordinary branch circuit found in the home. Such circuits are protected by a 15-ampere fuse or breaker, and portable tools draw only about 1 to 8 amperes. When other appliances and lighting fixtures share the circuit, however, a fuse may blow when a tool is turned on. A permanent solution is to install a separate line for a tool with a heavy current draw.

If you install a large stationary tool such as a table or radial arm saw the power source grows more important. In many instances, the tool is located in a basement workshop near the fuse or circuit breaker cabinet, where there is ample voltage and current. Some houses, however, have low line voltage—less than about 115; in other cases the tool may be located many rooms away from the fuse box. Both these factors can limit the tool's effectiveness. Manufacturers anticipate the problem by fitting heavy-duty tools with a provision for either 120 or 240 volts. Once the choice is made, a terminal inside a connection box can be correctly rewired. At 240 volts an electrical line of a given size suffers far less power loss and voltage drop than on 120 volts. Many homes already have 240-volt service, but it takes an electrician to run a branch circuit between the fuse box and power tool.

No matter how carefully a tool is designed, it sometimes needs attention and repair. Is this a do-it-yourself task? For basic maintenance the answer is yes. Inspection and replacement of the carbon brushes, a pair of slippery graphite blocks that carry electricity to the spinning parts of the motor, is usually done by removing a pair of screw-in caps on the housing. Some tools occasionally require a few drops of light machine oil in an access hole provided for the purpose. If a tool has a gear case, it should be periodically opened, cleaned of old grease, and repacked with fresh lubricant.

Since the advent of double insulation, manufacturers have grown wary of owner repair much beyond these basics. The problem is that a tool must be reassembled correctly to maintain its protective insulating qualities. Unless you're sure you know how to take apart and reassemble the tool correctly, take it to a local service station specified by the manufacturer. Whether you can do the job depends also on the instruction booklet. Some are marvels of clarity; others are cryptic documents of little value.

If you disassemble a tool, watch out for a possible trouble spot. Sleeve bearings, which support motor shafts, are sometimes held in place by split halves of the tool housing. Unless you reinstall those bearings with careful alignment, they may not be seated properly and will rub against the motor shaft. After the halves are tightened, be sure the shaft turns freely.

Two chores you should be able to do yourself are cleaning and tightening. Power tools are air-cooled, and long sessions of sawing or sanding stir up dust and wood chips that clog air vents on the housing. Keep those slots free of debris with a brush or stick. Retighten screws, nuts, and bolts regularly. They frequently loosen due to the vibration of power tool operation.

Carbon brushes are removable for inspection and replacement.

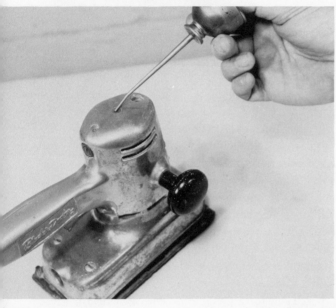

A few drops of light machine oil in motor bearing may occasionally be needed.

If a tool has a gear case, as in this saber saw, it will probably have to be cleaned and repacked with grease.

One important point for all maintenance and repair work: be sure to remove the power plug before any troubleshooting.

Throughout this book are dozens of operating and maintenance tips for power tools of any manufacture. Your tool's instruction sheet, however, contains the gospel for your model and should never be violated. If the manual or a local service station can't solve a problem, write to the company's customer service manager. Chances are he'll know (from complaining letters) about exotic troubles that aren't covered in the instructions. He may describe improvements made to the tool since you purchased it; these can sometimes be retrofitted to your model.

Check and tighten screws on tools that operate with considerable vibration.

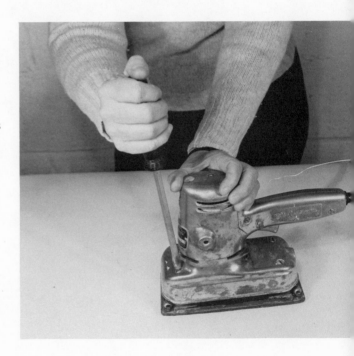

The art of working with tools originated about 700,000 years ago. Though flint artifacts have evolved into modern motorized tools, many basic cuts survive in much the same form. About a dozen of the important ones, mentioned frequently throughout this book, are illustrated here.

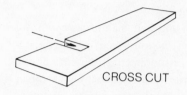
CROSS CUT

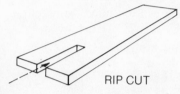
RIP CUT

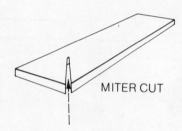
MITER CUT

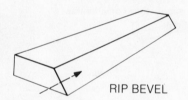
CROSS BEVEL

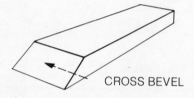
RIP BEVEL

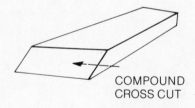
COMPOUND
CROSS CUT

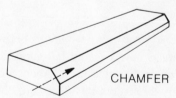
CHAMFER

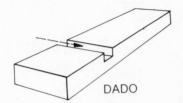

DADO

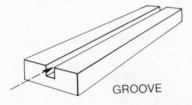

GROOVE

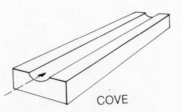

COVE

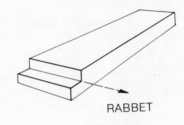

RABBET

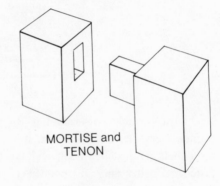

MORTISE and
TENON

Basic Saw Cuts

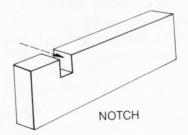

NOTCH

2
DRILL

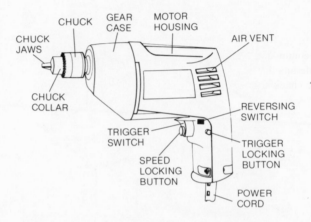

The most popular power tool is the portable electric drill. It is simple to operate, versatile, and a bargain. It is almost impossible to hang a curtain, put up a shelf, or install a hook without drilling a hole. The power drill does it faster and better than an ''eggbeater'' drill cranked by hand and costs only a little more than the manual model. An electric drill is highly recommended as the first power tool for a youngster getting started in model making or project building. There are many optional accessories available in the market that can be attached to the drill to multiply its usefulness.

THE BASIC DRILL

A typical portable model has a pistol grip with a trigger switch for controlling power. Inside the housing is an electric motor coupled to a gear train that converts the motor's high speed to fewer revolutions per minute at high twisting force. The drill's cutting tool is the *bit,* a removable part that slides into the three gripping jaws of the *chuck.*

The maximum opening of the chuck determines the drill's size: $1/4$ inch, $3/8$ inch, or $1/2$ inch. Most bits have a constant diameter from cutting tip to shank (the end that fits into the chuck), but there are exceptions. Wood bits, for example, can bore holes more than 1 inch wide, but they have a $1/4$-inch shank that fits the smallest drill. For cutting metal and other hard material, however, such oversize bits are not often practical because they can overload the motor of a small drill.

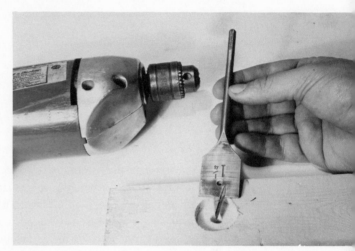

A drill can accommodate wood-boring or spade bits that flare wider than the chuck's opening.

The speed of a drill is related to chuck size. As bit capacity grows larger, drill speed decreases because large bits must turn more slowly to avoid the tremendous heat of friction they develop at high speeds. Large bits also demand the high torque (twisting force) made available by gearing down motor speed. Thus, maximum speeds of the three most popular drills run in this descending order: $1/4$-inch chuck, 1600 to 2200 rpm; $3/8$-inch chuck, 1000 rpm; $1/2$-inch chuck, 500 to 600 rpm.

CHOOSING A DRILL

The most popular model has been the single-speed $1/4$-inch size. It's still a good choice, but only if you plan to do mainly light drilling in soft materials like wood. It also performs well for narrow-diameter holes because these are done best at high speed, and a $1/4$-inch drill develops the highest of all. Do not, however, expect it to bore through masonry or turn heavy accessories.

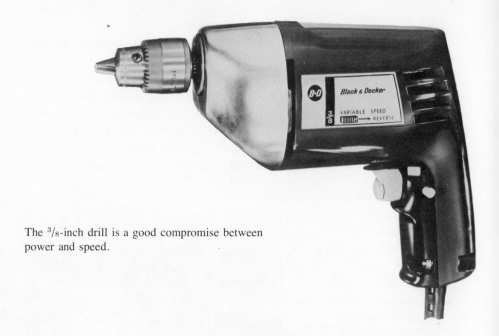

The ³/₈-inch drill is a good compromise between power and speed.

The massive ¹/₂-inch drill is rarely a good choice for an amateur. Very slow speed and high torque make it a specialized item for the professional. Consider it only if you regularly bore large holes in masonry, steel, tile, or other hard materials that require tremendous driving power. Another shortcoming is that the highest rpm of a ¹/₂-inch model is too slow for sanders, polishers, and other popular accessories.

The ³/₈-inch drill, which attempts to combine the speed of a ¹/₄-inch drill and the power of a ¹/₂-incher, is the best all-around choice for most home craftsmen. There are compromises involved in the use of any intermediate size, but a ³/₈-inch model handles a greater variety of bits and accessories than do other sizes. Another advantage is that ³/₈ inch is a common hole size for manufactured products, so you can use your ³/₈-incher for repairs or improvements to household items.

Variable-speed control is worth the modest extra cost. Starting a hole is easier with variable speed. You put the point of the bit on a pencil mark and gently squeeze the trigger until the motor starts. As the bit scores the work, you can gradually accelerate the drill to normal speed. If you attempt to start a hole in a smooth surface, such as sheet metal, with a high-speed drill, the bit may skitter out of control. A starting dimple made with a center punch is mandatory in applying a fixed-speed drill to slippery work, but a variable-speed drill makes this extra step unnecessary.

Another boon of variable speed is that a drill can be adjusted to match cutting conditions. A large bit, heavy pressure, and dense material conspire to generate damaging heat, which is reduced by decreasing the rpm. Note, though, that slowing the bit in a variable-speed drill does not increase its torque. Because the reduction is done electronically, not through mechanical gearing, it merely slows shaft speed without multiplying torque. Slower speeds, however, do lessen the heat generated in hard material.

A drill's *power* is not an unfailing index of its torque. Nameplates state horsepower or amperage, but actual power delivered to the bit is rarely quoted. Because different gears and bearings make exact comparisons difficult, check the manufacturer's informal category designation. "Industrial" or "contractor" signifies a tool intended for almost continuous operation. Some manufacturers classify a drill as light-, medium-, or heavy-duty. "Good," "better," and "best" are other guides to help you decide if a model is built for occasional use around the home, for a serious craftsman, or for a tradesman in his daily work. If no designation appears, the tool may be what the industry calls a "consumer" product, that is, one intended for light service.

Bearings reflect a tool's quality. Least expensive are sleeve bearings, followed in ascending order by needle, roller, and ball. Many designs mix types of bearings, using ball bearings where the load is heaviest. If you buy a model with low-cost bearings there will be a tendency for the tool to overheat under steady drilling. In this case the drill must be allowed to cool at frequent intervals. Low-cost bearings may be inconvenient but they're not a serious deficiency if the tool is used for only light-duty work.

A drill with double insulation usually has a plastic housing (dark area) and a metal gear compartment and chuck (at left).

With a screwdriver bit inserted in the drill chuck you can install hardware. Drills with reversing feature can remove screws or jammed hardware.

Several other features deserve attention. Double insulation is advisable for its protection against shock and the convenience of a 2-wire plug. Jammed bits are easier to extract if a drill has a *reversing lever,* which is also useful for unscrewing hardware with a screwdriver attachment. A *locking button* enables you to preset a drill for continuous rotation when you're using attachments like a wire brush or drill stand. Some models lock the motor only at the drill's highest-rpm mode; others hold it at any speed you select. Check if the tool's motor brushes—carbon blocks that eventually wear out—can be removed without completely disassembling the drill's main housing. In most models you merely remove two caps or a small section of the cover to inspect and replace the brushes.

Finally, heft the drill in your hand and judge its comfort. The handle shouldn't be too skimpy for your grip or have a slippery feel. The area where the handle emerges from the housing is important because it affects balance; if it is too far to the rear the tool will be nose-heavy and unwieldy. Determine if the trigger is comfortable to pull and the locking button easy to operate. A drill with a lock must be capable of rapid release so you can quickly turn off the motor in an emergency. Many drills have a tapped hole in the side of the case for an auxiliary handle. It provides a second handhold to help you drill with steadiness and accuracy.

The outer dimensions of a drill vary little from one model to the next and overall size is not usually significant. There are, however, compact models with a motor housing that's about half the diameter of a conventional drill. A compact could be a good choice if you store your drill in a case with other tools and carry it frequently from job to job in the field.

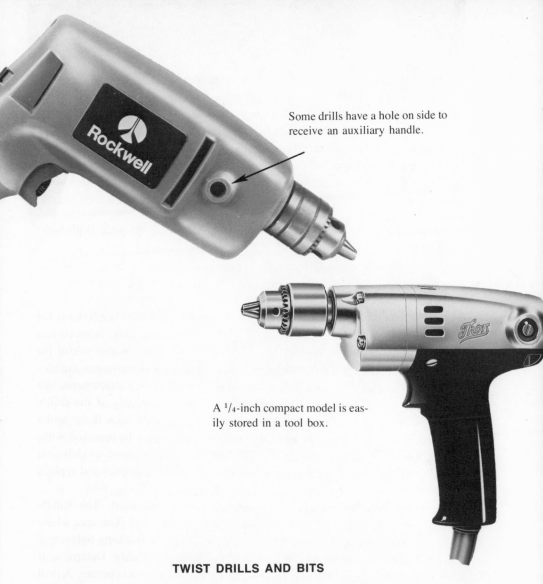

Some drills have a hole on side to receive an auxiliary handle.

A ¹/₄-inch compact model is easily stored in a tool box.

TWIST DRILLS AND BITS

These are sold in fractional sizes, which start at ¹/₁₆ inch and increase every ¹/₆₄ inch up to several inches in diameter. A good beginning assortment for a ¹/₄-inch drill is a 13-piece set that runs from ¹/₁₆ inch to ¹/₄ inch. For a ³/₈-inch drill, a good starter is a 21-piece set that ranges from ¹/₁₆ inch to ³/₈ inch. (Drill bits are also sold in 26 letter sizes, according to the alphabet, and in wire gauge sizes from No. 1 through No. 80. A set in fractional sizes, however, is ample for the beginner.)

Twist drills are sold in two grades: *high-speed* and *carbon steel*. The former, more expensive and widely available, are able to withstand the heat of drilling hard material. Carbon steel bits, on the other hand, are lower in cost but not inferior in quality—*unless* subjected to high heat. Either high-speed or carbon steel bits are adequate to bore holes in wood.

If you wish to make holes larger than the size of your drill chuck, you can purchase oversize bits. Remember, though, that large holes demand considerable power and the motor of a $^1/_4$-inch drill may be hard-pressed to drive a big bit. Spade bits, whose shank broadens into a wide, flat area that cuts neat holes in wood, are an exception. These bits cut well in soft wood at the high speeds of a $^1/_4$-inch or $^3/_8$-inch drill.

A set of *carbide-tipped* drills is a valuable accessory for the homeowner. Finished with an extremely hard material, these bits cut brick, stone, concrete, slate, and ceramic. Carbide bits must rotate at slow speeds, so don't expect them to cut effectively at the rapid rate of a fixed-speed $^1/_4$-inch drill.

ACCESSORIES

You can obtain drill attachments that do everything from trim a hedge and polish rocks to clear a clogged drain and shine your shoes. But don't expect all these minor miracles from a single drill because some accessories either won't work well on the drill's limited power or may be cumbersome to manipulate on that particular drill. Frequently an elaborate accessory is a poor substitute for an independent tool made expressly for the job. Before purchasing any attachments check the drill's instruction manual to see if the manufacturer has an approved-accessories list. The guarantee might be voided if the drill is overloaded or has its airflow blocked by an unapproved attachment.

Sanding-polishing kits are useful accessories. A disk sander is formed by inserting a rubber disk in the drill to serve as a flexible backing for sandpaper and other abrasives. With this flexible attachment you can sand irregular surfaces or remove paint. A *drum* sander can be fastened in the drill chuck for smoothing curved surfaces. There are also grinding wheels to sharpen tools and wire brushes to remove rust, paint, and dirt.

You can insert a flexible shaft into the drill chuck to extend the motive force by as much as 3 feet. With small bits attached to the end of the shaft (in dentist style) you can do fine work without wielding the whole weight of the drill. Large holes in wood, metal, or plastic are conveniently cut with a *hole saw* attachment. It is available in adjustable diameters, or as a set of individual blades that range in ten sizes from $^3/_4$ inch up to $2^1/_2$ inches. For extremely large holes—up to 12-inch circles—a *compass cutter* guides a cutting edge around the circumference in router fashion.

Drill attachments include wire wheels, at left; grinding wheels; and arbor, in hand, for attaching polishing wheels.

A rubber pad forms flexible backing of a disk sander attachment.

Buffing wheel attachment.

Wire brush drill attachment removes rust.

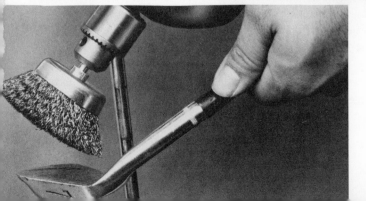

Typical twist drill bits: three high-speed steel bits at left, carbide-tipped bit in drill chuck, oversize bit in hand.

The carbide-tipped drill bit has an extra-hard cutting edge for making holes in brick and masonry.

Speed reduction devices are useful. They can slow a high-speed drill and improve its torque for drilling brick and other highly abrasive materials. Another special instrument is an *angle drill* head, which forms a right angle that places the working end of a drill into close quarters (between joists or rafters, for example). It also makes the drill easier to hold while sanding and polishing. To cut deep holes, as in a floor between rooms of a house, an *extension bit* is useful.

A handy new accessory is a *drill bit sharpener;* insert a worn bit into its opening and the device grinds it in pencil sharpener fashion.

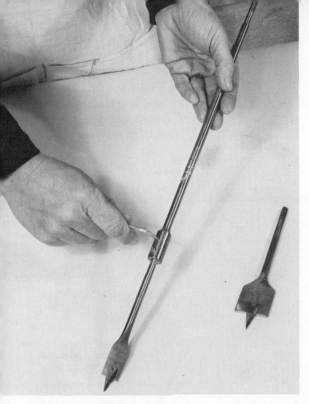

Drill bit extension for long reach. Upper end is clamped in drill chuck; lower end receives a conventional bit.

A hole saw attachment cuts larger openings than are possible with drill bits.

Compass cutter attachment mounted in chuck.

Drill bit sharpener. Bit is inserted in one of the holes in top and is ground by an internal wheel.

Drill stand converts a portable drill to a drill press.

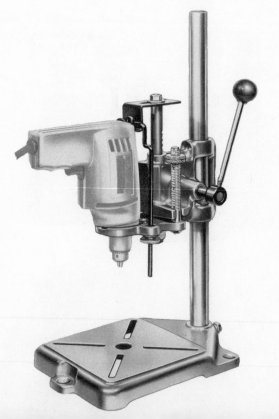

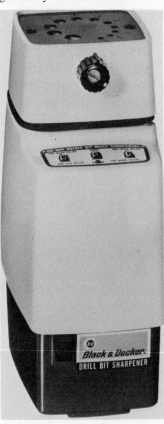

A particular convenience of the small electric drill is that you can bring it directly to the work. As you discover more uses for the tool, however, its portability may turn into a liability. And for many jobs on the bench, you won't be able to control the drill with precision. Sloppy holes often don't matter in a wall or rough lumber, but meticulous projects need accurate, controlled cuts. The *drill stand* is an excellent accessory to achieve precision. It converts a portable tool into a miniature drill press by holding the tool in a vertical position and allowing you to lower the bit with great accuracy and steadiness to a desired depth. A slightly different drill stand design holds a drill horizontally in the correct position for grinding, sharpening, or turning a wire brush.

DRILL PRESS

The full-fledged drill press, manufactured for industry, is mounted on a floor stand or tabletop base. It's such a versatile, supremely accurate tool that hobbyists occasionally buy it for home use, despite its high cost and massive proportions. With a wide range of speeds and interchangeable spindles, a drill press does a remarkable variety of metal-cutting, wood-boring, mortising, and other jobs. Work can be clamped in a vise at almost any angle and drilled to close tolerances and exact depths.

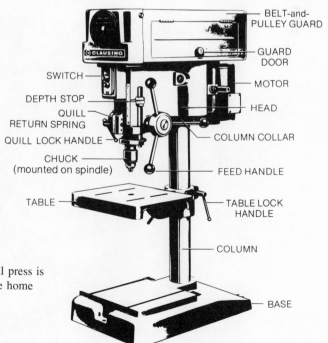

The industrial-type drill press is sometimes found in the home workshop.

SUGGESTED SPINDLE SPEEDS FOR DRILL PRESS (rpm)							
Hole Size (in.) *	Softwood	Hardwood	Plastic	Aluminum	Brass	Cast Iron	Mild Steel
$1/16$	4700	4700	4700	4700	4700	4700	2400
$1/8$	4700	4700	4700	4700	4700	2400	1250
$3/16$	4700	2400	2400	4700	2400	2400	1250
$1/4$	2400	2400	2400	4700	2400	1250	700
$5/16$	2400	1250	1250	2400	1250	1250	700
$3/8$	2400	1250	1250	2400	1250	700	700
$7/16$	2400	1250	1250	1250	1250	700	
$1/2$	1250	1250	1250	1250	700	700	
$5/8$	1250	700	700	700			
$3/4$	1250	700	700	700			
$7/8$	1250	700					
1	700	700					
$1 1/4$	700	700					
$1 1/2$	700	700					
2	700	700					

* For intermediate sizes use suggested speed for next-larger hole.
NOTE: Use a slower speed for a deep hole, or if drill bit burns or melts material.

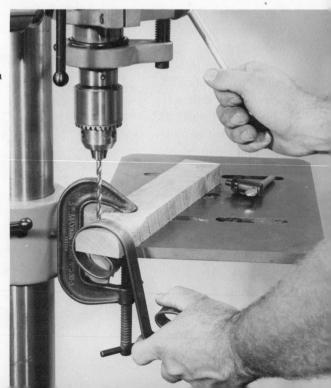

A drill press can be used to cut a hole in an iron bar, clamped against scrap wood.

A cylindrical piece is steadied for drilling by placing it in a V-block fixture. Additional support is gained from step block at left. Note slots in table for bolting fixtures.

The size of a drill press is the distance in inches between the center of its spindle and the front face of the supporting column multiplied by 2. Typical capacities run from sizes 11 to 15. The motor, generally purchased as a separate item, mounts on an adjustable bracket and is controlled by a stepped belt-and-pulley drive. The belt is shifted on the pulley to vary spindle speed.

There are signs that the drill press is making the transition from strictly commercial application to the home workshop. Until the nineteen-seventies the conventional drill press, a massive floor tool, was rarely found in the home. This changed when a 12-pound tabletop model with a $3/8$-inch chuck appeared on the market to fill the gap between the factory drill press and the clamp-on stand for a portable drill.

HOW TO USE A DRILL

The first step in operating a portable drill is installing the bit. Push it into the chuck as far as it will go, and carefully center it in the jaws as you tighten the chuck. Avoid inserting the bit off-center or it will wobble and probably break when it spins. Most chucks have three holes for tightening, and it's good

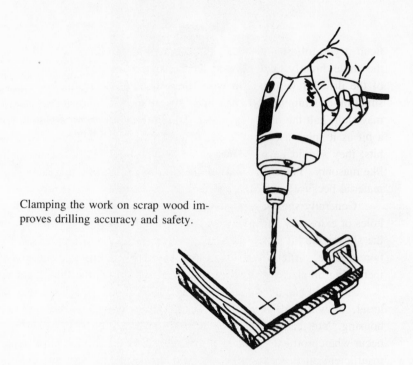

Clamping the work on scrap wood improves drilling accuracy and safety.

practice to insert the key and tighten all three jaws for maximum security. Never use a wrench to tighten the chuck—hand pressure on the chuck key is enough to secure the bit.

Unless the work is large or stationary, fasten it in a vise or clamp. Holding a small item in the hand may cause injury if it's suddenly seized by the bit and whirled from your grip. This is most likely to happen just before the bit breaks through the hole at the underside of the work. If you're working with a fixed-speed drill, especially a fast-turning $1/4$-inch model, first make a tiny dimple in the work with a center punch or even a nail. It reduces a bit's tendency to skid at the beginning of the job.

Never apply the spinning drill bit to the work; first put the bit on the mark, then pull the trigger. If the drill has variable speed, apply the bit and gently squeeze the trigger. As the barely turning bit scores the work, increase the speed.

Elaborate industrial charts tell the best cutting speed for each bit and type of material. These ratings are used in factory production because they create the neatest work with the least abuse of the tool. The amateur, however, faces a wide variety of cutting jobs with a single tool that must compromise speed with power. Yet choosing the proper rpm rate with a variable-speed drill is not difficult if you follow a few rules-of-thumb. With the bit applied to the work, eye the angle directly. You must apply the right amount of pressure along the line of the drill bit with no sidewise force; bending will almost certainly snap a small bit or strain the drill bearings. If you apply too much pressure, the motor may stall, halt the bit, or overheat. Too little pressure, on the other hand, dulls a bit as it spins uselessly in the hole. This is a critical problem with carbide bits; they should never be permitted to turn freely inside abrasive substances like masonry. You'll know when the drill is turning at a favorable speed in any material because you'll see and feel the bit cutting.

Generally speaking, high speeds are best for small holes, slow for larger holes or extremely abrasive work. Another guideline is: the harder the material, the slower the bit should turn. Soft materials require a high speed. When you bore a large, difficult hole, the job is eased by drilling a small hole first, then increasing bit size one or more times until you reach the final diameter.

Any drill can overheat. When drilling with heavy pressure, into dense material, or with an oversize bit, bearing friction radiates heat throughout the housing. You can feel and sometimes smell this heat. Overheating can also occur when protracted drilling at low rpm slows the cooling fan to a point where insufficient air is moved through the housing. If the drill becomes more than slightly warm to the touch, remove it from the work and operate the motor at its highest speed. This treatment is more efficient than letting the tool cool on the bench because cooling is more rapid when the fan turns at maximum speed while the drill is under no load.

Heat also develops at the point where the drill bit turns against the work. To reduce harmful effects, use some type of lubrication for difficult cutting jobs. Although not required for most light-duty work, a drop or two of oil at the point of the bit eases friction while cutting metal. Iron and brass, however, should be drilled dry. On aluminum, lubricate with turpentine or kerosene. For slate, masonry, ceramic, and other material drilled with a carbide bit, water is a good medium to reduce friction.

When a drill bit jams, stop the tool immediately. A drill with variable speed and a reversing feature is easiest to free if you slowly back out of the hole, encouraging the bit to release with short bursts of power. Never operate the reversing lever until the motor stops turning forward. When operating in reverse, watch out for overheating; the fan may not pull enough air in this direction for more than a brief period.

Be wary of potentially dangerous situations while operating a drill. You could inadvertently poke a bit into a wall and slice a live electrical cable. There is an increasing possibility of this as more homebuilders convert from steel-armored cable (BX) to plastic-coated wire (Romex). If the bit strikes a "hot" conductor the grounding feature of a 3-wire cable, on older drills, or double insulation, on newer ones, should provide ample personal protection. You can avoid trouble by first drilling only through the wall panel (a depth of $3/4$ inch or less), until the bit just breaks through. Then insert an insulated screwdriver into the cavity and feel for wires, plumbing, or other obstructions that may block the bit.

Another hazard is a drill bit jamming to a stop inside the work. A $1/4$-inch drill would probably stall in this instance, but a more powerful motor could twist the tool out of your hand. A quick trigger release should end the danger—but not if the trigger is locked when the bit seizes. Be alert for this possibility; don't use the lock when drilling in tough material or deep holes, or if the bit is dull. The risk in deep holes is reduced if you frequently back out the bit to allow sawdust or chips to flow out of the hole. And once again, be sure to clamp the work securely if this can be done.

MAINTAINING THE DRILL

Fortunately drills require little maintenance. Many have gears and bearings which are lubricated for life. Check the manufacturer's instructions. He may recommend that you bring the tool to a service center once a year for cleaning and lubrication. One company suggests a three- to six-month interval for such servicing, but this schedule may be too frequent for a drill that's used only a few hours each month.

Many modern drills never require grease repacking in the gear case because the compartment is well protected against leakage and foreign matter. Some drills, on the other hand, have a small hole on the case to lubricate motor bearings. Apply about three drops of machine oil occasionally, but resist the temptation to overdo it. Excess lubricant may leak onto electrical contacts and burn the copper surfaces.

The components most prone to wear—the brushes—are usually serviceable by the owner. Pressing against a spinning commutator, the brushes act as sliding electrical contacts and wear each time the drill operates. If permitted to erode to less than $1/4$ inch, they can slow or stop the motor. Brushes are easy to inspect and replace (see page 11), but first remove the plug from the wall outlet to prevent any shock hazard.

An aging drill often suffers wear and deterioration of its commutator, a ring of copper bars that contacts the brushes. Through sparking and mechanical force, the brushes wear grooves into the soft copper and oxidize it, darkening its surface. Both conditions, visible after brushes are removed, gradually slow the drill and decrease its power. Minor cases of rough or blackened commutator bars can be treated by cleaning with No. 3/0, or finer, sandpaper. Never use emery cloth because its metal particles can short-circuit the insulated segments between the commutator bars. If the commutator is deeply grooved and pitted, return it to the service center for "turning down." In this case the copper surface is placed in a lathe and renewed by a cutting tool.

Ventilation is crucial to the maintenance of a drill and important for safety as well. If air holes are choked, the tool will overheat and possibly damage its electrical insulation. Prevent problems by cleaning vent openings with a brush or thin length of wood. Occasionally wipe the line cord clean so oil and grease can't attack the insulation and increase shock hazard. Electric drills need little service—but caring for these details every six months or so will keep the tool in top working order.

3
SABER SAW

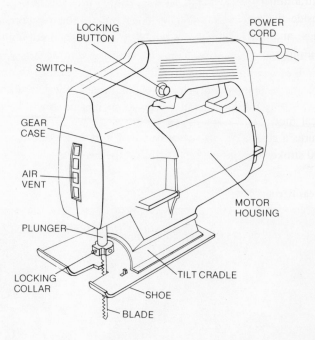

LOCKING BUTTON

SWITCH

GEAR CASE

AIR VENT

PLUNGER

LOCKING COLLAR

POWER CORD

MOTOR HOUSING

TILT CRADLE

SHOE

BLADE

After the electric drill, the saber saw is one of the most popular power tools sought by home craftsmen. Some manufacturers call it a "jigsaw," others a "bayonet," but we'll use "saber," a name that appears to be gaining in favor over the others. Whatever the name, it is an electrified version of the old-fashioned handsaw in which the blade is powered back and forth. The tool is easy to manipulate and light enough to carry to the work.

But the saber saw is more than a motorized handsaw. A thin blade anchored at one end confers a remarkable ability to follow intricate curves and contours. With the right blade, the tool cuts cardboard, wood, plastic, metal, leather, ceramic, asphalt, or rubber tile.

Some tasks are not particularly suited to the saber saw. The narrowness of the blade sacrifices speed and precision in extended straight cuts. Straight edges are done more rapidly and evenly using a circular or table saw. Other limitations are in cutting depth and length. If the stock is more than 2 inches thick or the guideline is long, a saber saw is tedious to operate. Although the saber saw can occasionally rip and cross-cut, a major project goes many times faster with the wide blade of a circular, table, or radial arm saw.

However, within its province—cutting through twists and turns—the saber saw is supreme. In addition to an ability to follow tortuous guidelines, it performs an extraordinary feat known as the *plunge cut*. The tool can start its own hole inside the area of a panel. It is thus ideal for making cut-outs in walls, ceilings, and other surfaces to mount outlets, boxes, and fixtures, or to run plumbing pipes.

THE BASIC SABER SAW

A typical model has a brush-type motor of about $1/6$ to $1/2$ horsepower. The motor turns a gear assembly to convert shaft rpm to a blade speed of about 2000 to 4000 strokes per minute (spm). Inside the housing, above the blade, is

A saber saw easily cuts curves.

An oversize blade can be used to cut through thick material.

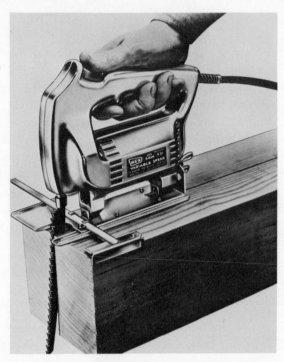

a wheel with an eccentric stud to transform rotary motion into reciprocating action that pulls a plunger up and down. The blade is fastened to a collar on the plunger with set screws, for quick changing.

The length of the blade determines the thickness of material a saber saw can cut. With a 3-inch blade you should be able to saw through a 2-inch-thick piece of lumber. Install a 4-inch blade, and the thickness you can cut increases to approximately $2^{1}/_{2}$ inches. There are also oversize blades to negotiate material as thick as 6 inches. Regardless of length, most blades have a $^{1}/_{4}$-inch shank which fits into the locking collar.

An important section of the saw is the shoe, or baseplate. Pressed against the work, its broad surface helps to keep the blade aligned. It prevents the work from vibrating and allows the blade teeth to bite into the material.

SPECIAL FEATURES

With a *tilting* shoe, the blade can be angled from the saw's base for bevel cuts. Another improvement is the *sliding* shoe. For normal cutting, the shoe is kept in a position forward of the blade, where it forms an overhang to support the tool when you begin a cut. Then, as you work, you can temporarily move the shoe to the rear of the tool and cut closer to a vertical surface.

Saw is tilted on shoe for bevel cutting.

Bevel scale on shoe (see arrow) permits blade to be preset at a desired angle.

Large scrolling knob at top allows blade to be rotated to follow a tight corner.

A saber saw model with variable speed and double insulation.

Removable insert, in blade slot at lower right, narrows gap for smooth cutting.

A conventional saber blade moves up and down in a vertical line. With *orbital action,* it travels a slightly different path: on the upstroke, the teeth move forward and bite into the material; on the downstroke, the blade retreats slightly to clear the cut and dissipate dust. The result is faster cutting, easier feed, and longer blade life.

In routine cutting, a saw is guided around curves by steering the handle with your hand. A *scrolling* feature lets you rotate the blade separately to make the job even easier. It enables the blade to turn tight corners, where swinging the whole tool might be difficult. Some models add the scrolling feature through a top knob controlled by hand; other designs put the blade in a free-swiveling mount that responds to changes in hand pressure. For straight cuts the blade is locked.

Variable speed in a saber saw enables you to apply gradual pressure to the trigger to start the blade from zero strokes per minute to a maximum of about 3000 spm. Some models have a *sawdust blower* to keep the cutting line clear and easy to see.

CHOOSING A SABER SAW

Wield the tool you want to buy, because you'll want handling ease for sustained cutting. If there's no separate handle and the tool is grasped by its housing, it may prove uncomfortable for lengthy sawing sessions. Some models have extra handles at the top or side to improve your steadiness and control. If you are permitted to try a prospective model, note the amount of vibration transmitted to your fingers. The plunger should be counterbalanced, but its effectiveness varies from one model to the next. For heavy use you'll want a tool with low vibration.

An all-metal construction improves a tool's durability but sacrifices some convenience because metal models are equipped with a 3-wire cord to eliminate shock hazard. That means you'll need a grounding outlet or adapter for safety. The plastic housing of a double-insulated saber saw eliminates that bother. Another benefit of plastic over metal is quieter operation.

Other items that suggest superior quality in a saber saw are ball or needle bearings in the motor and gear case. They develop less friction than do the common sleeve bearings standard on most models. Choose better bearings if you plan to use the saw for protracted periods of serious work. A well-designed saw also has easily accessible carbon brushes. In the simplest arrangement two caps on the housing are unscrewed to reveal the brushes. Other saws require partial disassembly of the housing.

The overhang of a saw's shoe—the part that protrudes forward of the blade—deserves careful inspection. If there's less than about $1/2$ inch of overhang, the shoe may not readily catch the edge of the work and could slip off. Too much overhang, on the other hand, prevents the blade from getting close to obstructing or vertical surfaces. That last deficiency isn't important if the shoe has the sliding feature.

Look at the width of the slot surrounding the blade. It should be narrow enough so that the shoe can exert firm pressure on the work and reduce the amount of splintering along the cut edges. Too narrow a slot, however, makes it difficult to see and follow the guideline in front of the blade or to remove a short piece from the end of a wood strip. Some manufacturers overcome this problem by supplying inserts that can be slipped into the slot whenever the work requires very smooth edges.

You can use additional clues to judge a saw's capacity. As for most tools, horsepower is only an approximate guide to force; cutting ability also depends on gears, bearings, and other variable factors that make close comparisons difficult. To state capacity without considering horsepower, a manufacturer may specify the tool's depth of cut according to type of material—for example: $1^5/8$ inches in softwood (the short dimension of a trimmed two-by-four); 1 inch in hardwood; $1/4$ inch in soft metal; and $1/4$ inch in steel.

Frequently a saber saw, like other "consumer" power tools, is described in a general category such as "light-duty" or "heavy-duty." The blade of a light-duty tool usually has a $1/2$-inch or $5/8$-inch stroke, while heavy-duty models have a 1-inch stroke. By spreading more teeth over the work in a greater stroke, the heavy-duty blade remains sharp longer. A heavy-duty model also has a huskier motor that draws about 4 amps (as opposed to about $2^1/2$ amps in a lighter model) for more motive force. The choice depends on the work you'll do. A small saw is easy to manipulate, handy for light wood-working tasks around home or shop. The heavy-duty model does them faster and tackles thicker material with its extra-length blade, but is more expensive and less agile. Metal-cutting blades, especially, last longer in a big saber saw because of the lengthy stroke.

There is a wide choice of speed controls in saber saws. In the simplest arrangement, a *single-speed* switch turns on the motor at full speed. It limits the tool mostly to working in relatively soft material. It also reduces the price. A locking button usually accompanies the switch to hold the motor continuously on. Both control switch and locking button should be easily accessible for quick release to stop the tool instantly.

A *two-speed* saw is the next step up. Since blade speed should vary with the job, a double-speed control broadens the tool's versatility and equips it to

	Wood	Compo-sition	Light Metal	Plexiglass	Plastic	Laminate	Heavy Metal	Scroll Cutting
Single-Speed								
Two-Speed								
Variable-Speed								

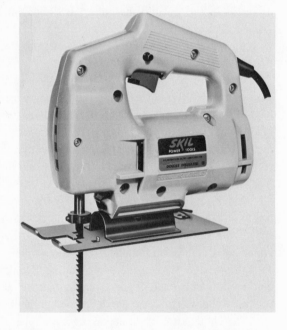

Locking button, to keep saw operating without finger pressure, is located in handle, just above trigger.

tackle tougher cutting jobs at slower speed. Some models have a *three-speed* control to refine the cutting action even more.

Variable speed enhances the saw's versatility further. Controlled by finger pressure on a trigger, a variable-speed saw is easier to start in a cut and to control and guide through the work. You can match cutting speed to the material, to avoid charring wood, for instance, or damaging the blade.

Most saber saws accept a large variety of blades, so long as they have a ¹/₄-inch shank to fit the locking collar. A saw may, however, be designed to accept only the blades of its manufacturer. The assortment may be ample to cope with any job, but check before you buy to see if you can conveniently obtain replacement blades or new types at a future time.

HOW TO USE A SABER SAW

The most dangerous area of a saber saw is at the plunger. If a finger is poked between plunger and shoe, it could be injured. This hazard is easy to avoid, however, because there is no reason to bring your hand near the plunger, blade, or shoe while the saw is running.

Manufacturers use a variety of methods to fasten a blade to the plunger. Usually the teeth of the blade face away from the saw, and the shank is inserted as far as it will go into the collar. It's especially important to insert *hollow-ground* blades all the way into the collar so their teeth will always make contact with the work. If you're replacing a broken blade, remove any shattered pieces that are lodged inside the collar.

Whenever possible, clamp the work or secure it in a vise. A saber saw vibrates forcefully, and its cutting motion is wasted if the work jitters with the blade. This problem occurs most often when you saw flexible material. The blade may appear to cut but makes little progress through the work. The remedy is to secure the material and exert firm pressure on the handle. To reduce splintering of the good side of the work, place that surface down, facing away from the blade.

A cut with a saber saw is started by placing the front overhang of the shoe firmly on the work and turning on the motor *before* the blade contacts the material. If the saw has a speed control, begin at the slowest rate until the tool is under good control and aligned with the guideline. Advance the saw with just enough pressure to keep the blade cutting. Don't push hard, or the blade may bind or slow down and cause a rough edge. Never twist the blade inside the cut because the powerful leverage developed at the handle is apt to snap the blade.

The choice of a blade depends on the type of work and its thickness. The more teeth per inch (tpi), the smoother will be the cut. Cutting with a fine blade, however, takes more time than with a coarser blade. You might choose a blade with 10 tpi for a smooth cut in fine work, one with 5 to 7 tpi for faster sawing of rough lumber. Metal cutting using thin sheet stock requires very close teeth—about 24 to 32 tpi. If fine teeth tend to clog when cutting soft metal, install a blade with fewer tpi. Cutting thick metal is done with a blade of about 14 to 24 tpi. Pick a wide blade for long, straight cuts, a narrow one for curves.

RECOMMENDED BLADE SELECTION FOR SABER SAW			
Application	Blade Width (in.)	Length of Cutting Edge (in.)	Teeth per Inch
Cutting fiberglass ($^1/_2$ inch thick or less)	$^3/_8$	$1^3/_8$	6
Rough-cutting wood	$^3/_8$	$2^3/_8$	6
Cutting softwood (up to 2 inches thick)—for fine-finish applications; not for scrollwork	$^1/_4$	3	7
Cutting hardwood or thin pieces (less than $^3/_4$ inch thick)	$^1/_4$	3	10
Cutting green or wet wood ($^3/_{16}$ to $1^5/_{16}$ inches thick); blade narrows toward shank for easier maneuvering	$^1/_4$	3	10
Scrollwork and general wood cutting	$^1/_4$	$2^3/_8$	10
Cutting intricate circles and other scrollwork in wood and plastic ($^1/_4$ to 1 inch thick)	$^1/_4$	$2^1/_2$	14
Cutting brass, bronze, copper, and other non-ferrous metals ($^5/_{16}$ to $^1/_2$ inch thick)	$^3/_8$	$2^1/_2$	10
Cutting brass, bronze, copper, and other non-ferrous metals ($^5/_{32}$ to $^1/_4$ inch thick)	$^3/_8$	$2^1/_2$	14
Cutting angle iron and mild-steel sheet and tubing ($^5/_{32}$ to $^1/_8$ inch thick)	$^1/_4$	$1^1/_4$	14
Cutting ferrous metal ($^1/_{64}$ to $^3/_{32}$ inch thick)	$^1/_4$	3	32
Cutting steel sheet and tubing ($^3/_{32}$ to $^1/_8$ inch thick)	$^3/_8$ $^1/_4$	$2^1/_2$ $1^1/_4$	24 24
Cutting cardboard, cloth, leather, and rubber	$^5/_{16}$	$1^7/_{16}$	0 (knife)
General wood cutting; cutting asphalt tile, fiber, paper and plastic laminates, linoleum, Lucite, nylon, plexiglass, and rubber	$^3/_8$ $^3/_8$	$2^3/_8$ 3	10 10

Short-distance or curved cuts are done merely by drawing a guideline on the work and steering the saw blade by eye. If you want greater accuracy, you'll need a guide. The simplest technique is to locate the blade on the guideline, then tack or clamp a straightedge on the work, using the side of the saw shoe as a reference. Now you can operate the saw with precision by sliding the shoe along the guide.

A short wood dowel is clamped in vise for sawing. Don't hold small pieces in hand.

Sawing through thin metal stock requires a closely toothed blade.

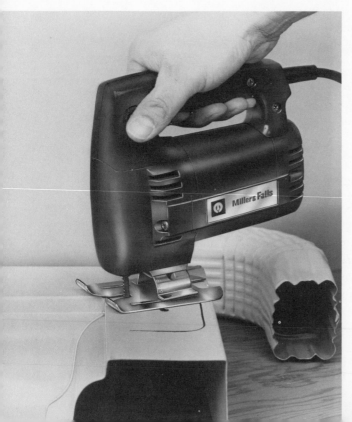

Straightedge clamped on work guides saw.

Rip guide, attached to saw shoe, rides along edge of work at right.

Using a saber saw for notch cutting.

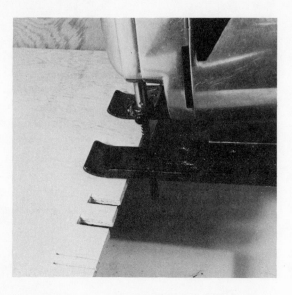

Either circular or straight cutting is neatly done with a *rip guide*. Accurate straight cuts are done by engaging the rip guide over the edge of the work (see illustration). By nailing one end of the guide to the center of an outlined circle (in a hole provided for the purpose), you can pivot the saw in a circle up to about 1 foot in diameter. There's a tendency for the blade to bind as it nears the end of a circular cut, but this is eased by inserting a wedge or two to widen the cut in that area. Choose a wide blade with few tpi for narrow circles because it cuts a roomy swath and thus turns easier in the material. Notch cutting in the edge of a panel is quickly done by making two sawcuts to the desired depth, then removing the tab with a chisel.

Plunge cutting with a saber saw.

To make a plunge cut, start by sliding the shoe to the forward position, if it is adjustable. The front of the shoe will act as a pivot point. Tilt the saw forward on the shoe's front edge and, with the blade clear of the work, turn on the power. Slowly rotate the saw *backward* to lower the blade into the work. Once the blade reaches full depth, start cutting the guideline in normal fashion.

A saber saw makes right angle cuts needed to square off a cut-out. It's done by moving the blade to a corner and stopping at the intersecting line. Back up a bit, then guide the blade in a curve until it again hits the intersecting line. After you've turned the four corners the piece falls out, allowing you room to cut the tiny bit of excess wood remaining in each corner.

TYPES OF BLADES

There are many special blades for saber saws. Because the life of any blade is shortened by abuse, such as application to abrasive or exceptionally hard material, the least expensive solution is to purchase a liberal blade assortment. The single most popular blade for most rough-cutting jobs in wood is the *saw set*—sometimes called *alternate set* because alternate teeth are spread left and right. A blade of about 6 tpi is suitable for material more than 1 inch thick; one of about 10 tpi is recommended for under 1 inch. (Note that a saw with less than a 1-inch stroke, even if fitted with an oversize blade, may not be powerful enough to cut thick lumber.)

Another blade category is *hollow-ground*. Its teeth lie in a straight line, with part of the blade ground away to reduce thickness. It makes very smooth, narrow cuts, but don't use one for curves. Special blades for cutting plywood have hollow-ground teeth that also make smooth cuts in plastic, Masonite, or linoleum. *Scroll* blades, which are narrow and flexible, are superior for intricate curves in thin plywood and other such material.

Metal-cutting blades are fabricated of high-strength steel for durability at high speeds. A common size is 32 tpi, with the teeth aligned in an undulating *wave set*. To cut heavy metal stock, choose a blade with fewer teeth—about 24 tpi. When cutting thin sheet metal, avoid curling of the material by sandwiching it between two sheets of thin plywood and following guidelines drawn on the wood. This clamping technique also prevents thin metal from oscillating with the blade and thereby neutralizing the cutting action. In any metal-cutting job keep speed at the lowest practical rate to prevent overheating and ruining the blade.

Another specialized blade is the *Teflon-coated* type. It's more expensive than conventional blades, but it generates less friction and can follow sharper curves. Foreign matter is less likely to stick to these blades as well. For cutting cardboard, leather, and rubber tile, use a *knife*-type blade made expressly for the purpose. One of the most difficult cutting jobs of all, slicing through ceramic tile or slate, is practical with *tungsten-carbide* blades. There are no teeth on these blades; they advance through the work with an abrasive action. They'll even cut through wood harboring concealed nails, a process that quickly ruins the teeth of a conventional blade. Cutting action is slow, but tungsten-carbide blades solve formidable cutting problems.

MAINTAINING THE SABER SAW

The life of a saw motor is shortened by heat, so be sure the tool's air vents remain open. Disconnect the power cord and remove clogged sawdust with a brush or stick. After several hours of operation (which may occur over several

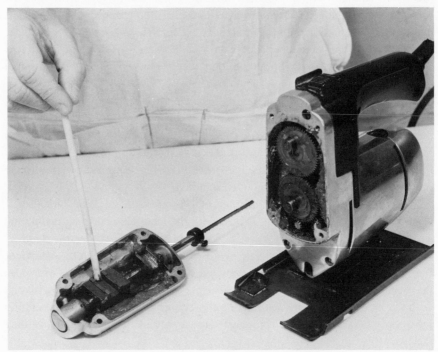

Front of gear case removed for lubrication. Pointer shows counterweight, which reduces vibration of plunger and blade.

weeks or in a single weekend) place a few drops of light machine oil into the holes, if provided, at the rear of the housing, which lead to the motor bearing. In some models you can remove the front plunger housing and oil the felt pads found there. Grease retained inside the case keeps gears and front bearings amply lubricated for long periods, but some manufacturers recommend a clean-out every 100 hours of operation, or whenever worn gears or bearings are replaced. Wipe out the old grease, flush the residue with kerosene, then refill the case two thirds full with gear grease.

When you reassemble a saber saw with a housing that splits evenly apart, be cautious with sleeve bearings situated between the two halves. These bearings must be carefully positioned when the tool is put back together to prevent poor alignment and excessive friction. Also be certain the line cord is correctly placed and not pinched when bolting together the housing.

Inspecting carbon brushes for wear is an easy task on most saber saws. Minimum brush length is $1/4$ inch to prevent power loss or possible damage to the motor commutator. If the tool has a troublesome solid-state speed control, this is a repair for a service dealer.

4

CIRCULAR SAW

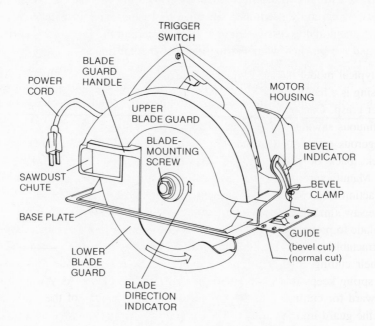

TRIGGER
SWITCH

BLADE
GUARD
HANDLE

POWER
CORD

MOTOR
HOUSING

UPPER
BLADE GUARD

BLADE-
MOUNTING
SCREW

BEVEL
INDICATOR

SAWDUST
CHUTE

BEVEL
CLAMP

BASE PLATE

GUIDE
(bevel cut)
(normal cut)

LOWER
BLADE
GUARD

BLADE
DIRECTION
INDICATOR

"Frame a cottage or add a room in a matter of days—hand sawing would take weeks!" That's how one tool manufacturer describes the prodigious capability of a circular saw. It's no exaggeration. The circular saw is a formidable tool that mutiplies your muscle power more than a dozen times. Even a novice can make straight cuts with clean, squared-off edges after a few trials. Team the tool with a saber saw, and you're equipped to tackle almost any carpentry job.

Portability is one reason why the circular saw enjoys enduring popularity among carpenters. Despite its power—it slices rafters, joists, studs, and other framing members—it can be carried by hand. Use one in the home and you won't have to carry unwieldy panels or long planks from one place to another or try to maneuver them into the restricted space around a table or radial arm saw. Awkward jobs that once took four hands to complete are quickly done by one person and a circular saw.

Don't expect the circular saw to cut intricate curves or small holes. That's the province of a saber saw. A circular saw excels at long, straight cuts at great speed. If you plan any major home improvements or serious carpentry, a circular saw is a wise investment.

THE BASIC CIRCULAR SAW

A typical model has an elongated housing with a 1- to 2-hp motor. Atop the housing is a handle with an on-off trigger switch that falls within your natural finger grasp. Conspicuously missing are a locking button to hold the tool on for continuous sawing, and a control to vary motor speed. A locking button is too dangerous on a tool that delivers the high speed of a circular saw. If the saw kicks back or slips, you can instantly remove power by releasing the trigger. Manufacturers have not installed slow-speed controls because the fast cutting action of a circular saw depends on high blade speed.

The saw's motor housing flares out to form a blade guard enclosing the top of the blade to prevent injury to the operator. Underneath, the blade is covered by a retractable guard assembly that protects you from spinning teeth but exposes their cutting edge at the proper moment. Before the blade touches the work a spring keeps this tooth guard pressed over the blade. As you push the saw forward for cutting, a lip on the guard catches the edge of the work; this retracts the guard into the housing. When you remove the saw, the guard automatically snaps back over the blade. This is important because the blade continues to spin for several seconds after the switch is turned off.

The most important dimension of a circular saw is the diameter of its blade, which may range from about 5 to 10 inches. The most popular choices fall midway between these extremes. The huge cross section of the blade, as compared with a saber saw, exerts a great steadying effect that keeps the tool cutting in a straight line.

All models have a baseplate that's adjustable in two ways for supporting the tool on the work. The base may be raised or lowered to control depth of the cut, or it may be set at an angle for bevel cuts.

Lower blade guard retracts as blade advances through the work.

Loosening wing nut allows blade to move vertically for adjusting depth of cut.

Bevel cutting is achieved by locking baseplate at desired angle with respect to the work.

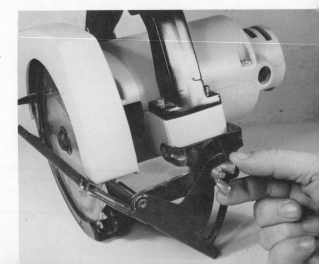

SPECIAL FEATURES

Circular saws with *double insulation* for electrical safety and operating convenience are available. A *slip clutch* is an additional feature found in some models; if the blade strikes an obstruction or is jammed in a cut, the clutch slips and prevents heat damage to the motor. A *lock-off* button, also called a *safety switch,* prevents a major hazard of the circular saw: when you grasp the handle to pick up the tool, you may inadvertently pull the trigger and turn on the motor. The safety switch prevents this because you must first disengage it before starting.

Slip clutch system. Blade is positioned between two clutch washers. A wrench is used to tighten bolt a half turn beyond finger-tight to attain proper slipping torque.

On some models a *riving knife* is fitted behind the blade. It holds the cut, or kerf, slightly apart to prevent the blade from binding, a handy feature when cutting green wood. Since a riving knife interferes with certain sawing operations, such as plunge cutting, it's removable.

In the electrical section of the saw, the manufacturer may provide a special carbon brush arrangement. In this case a brush that's worn below a safe thickness cannot make contact with, and therefore damage, the commutator, which is rotating on the motor shaft. Another electrical item is an *electronic brake*. By setting up opposing magnetic fields in the motor windings, it quickly slows the shaft to a stop after the trigger is released. Saws without this feature take several moments to slow down from a top speed of about 5500 rpm.

CHOOSING A CIRCULAR SAW

Unless you're engaged in heavy work, you'll probably select a tool in the midrange of price, size, and power. At the high end are 2-hp commercial-duty saws of $10^1/_4$ inches, but these are hardly suitable for home use. The smallest saws are in the $^3/_4$-hp category with a blade of about 5 inches. One of the most common and practical sizes for the handyman is $7^1/_4$ inches. It cuts through just about any thickness you're likely to encounter, including the important 2-inch dimension of framing members (studs, rafters, etc.). Exact cutting capacities are often stated by the manufacturer, as in a typical $7^1/_4$-inch model: $2^7/_{16}$ inches at 90 degrees (the conventional cutting angle); $1^7/_8$ inches at 45 degrees (for slanting, or bevel, cuts).

If a $7^1/_4$-inch blade is ample for your needs but you want maximum cutting speed, buy a model with high horsepower. Motors are available in a range from about 1 to 2 hp. Another way to beef up the tool for heavy work is to purchase a model with ball or roller bearings. Such bearings generate less friction than do the sleeve bearings commonly found in noncommercial models.

The saw's baseplate deserves special scrutiny. You'll want a rigid support to bear the tool's weight. Heavy-duty models have a wrap-around base that sur-

Larger models often have a wrap-around baseplate that supports the tool on both sides of blade.

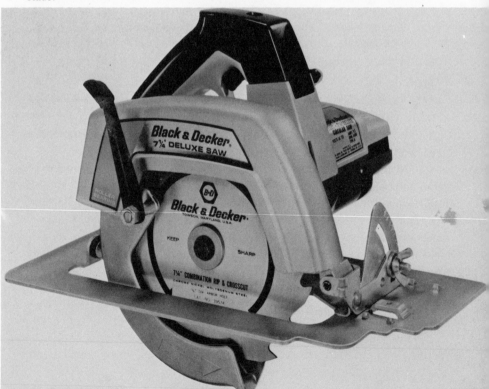

Auxiliary handle (see arrow) provides a second holding grip to steady a heavy-duty circular saw.

rounds the blade on both sides. Look also in the baseplate area for one or more guides that help you steer the tool along a line marked on the work. Is the guide clearly visible when you stand in the operating position? Study the baseplate adjustments for depth and bevel cuts. It's helpful to have an easy-to-see reference calibrated in degrees for bevel cuts.

Lift the tool, concentrating on grip and balance. The saw may weigh from 9 to 13 pounds. If the handle is not well designed, your hand could grow tired during long sawing sessions, even though the tool's weight rests on the work. On some heavy models an auxiliary handle helps you maneuver and steady the saw.

Has the designer provided any other valuable improvements? Following a pencil mark on the work is easier if the motor's air blast also blows sawdust off the guideline to keep it visible. Did he consider ease of brush replacement? Some models let you examine brushes without opening the housing; others require considerable dismantling. This isn't a critical item, but it's a convenience that could sway you toward one tool over another.

TYPES OF BLADES

Circular saws are customarily fitted at the factory with a *combination blade,* which is the best compromise for all-around work. It does a satisfactory job in either cross cutting (sawing across the grain) or ripping (where the blade runs with the grain of the wood). When it's time to purchase a replacement, one improvement would be a combination blade with a plastic coating, which reduces friction and speeds the cutting action. If you plan to do extensive cross or rip cutting, consider a specialized blade for smoother results: a *cross cut blade* has finer teeth; a *rip blade* has a tooth design that ensures a fast, smooth cut with the grain.

A *plywood blade,* another special type, cuts more slowly than does a combination blade, but its finer teeth produce smoother edges in plywood. A *metal-cutting blade,* with an aluminum oxide surface, slices through both ferrous and nonferrous metals. Sometimes a blade is tipped with carbide for hardness, or coated with Teflon for self-lubrication—two improvements that further lower friction. For exceptionally fine work, where you want to achieve smooth end

CIRCULAR SAW BLADES

FLOORING

LIGHT-GAUGE METAL AND FIBERGLASS

PLYWOOD

COMBINATION

CROSS CUT

HARDWOOD, PLASTIC, AND NONFERROUS METAL

HOLLOW-GROUND

CARBIDE-TIPPED

Rip guide rides along side of stock to keep cut straight and accurate.

grain cuts on trim or in cabinet making, look into a *planer blade*. A *flooring blade* has the tough edge needed to slice through wood that might conceal nails.

A variety of other blades rely solely on abrasive action to eat their way through materials that would wreck an ordinary blade. Sometimes called *cutoff wheels,* they cut through metal, brick, cinder block, tile, concrete block, and wallboard. Despite the tenacity of these blades, be careful to avoid sidewise pressure. The rigid, abrasive material they're made of is embedded in a flexible disk, and side stress could cause the blade to shatter. Keep the pressure light and don't twist the saw handle.

After blades, there are few accessories for a circular saw. A *rip guide* is an excellent attachment, as is a *saw protractor* to accurately guide a cut at any angle from 0 to 90 degrees.

HOW TO USE A CIRCULAR SAW

Keep your wits about you when working with a circular saw. The same factors that make it a masterful tool present a potential danger. Although the noise of motor and teeth biting through the material gives fair warning, the blade is concealed by the guard and out of your line of sight. That's why it's important to visualize where the blade is at every moment—and *never* to put your hand at the underside of the work.

Some simple safety rules for a circular saw vastly reduce any hazard. When changing blades, first remove the plug from the wall. Don't attempt to saw small pieces while holding them in your hand; use a clamp. Don't use a dull blade because it burns the work or, worse, kicks back. Be ready to release the trigger instantly on a kickback. Never pull the saw backward through wood with the blade spinning—you might lose control. To reverse direction, instead remove the saw from the work and turn it around.

When you install a blade in the tool, watch out for certain details. Most saws have arrows marked on the blade and on the blade guard to show direction of rotation. It's essential that teeth turn in an upward sweep from under the work, so be sure the arrows agree. If the blade has a slip clutch and you over-tighten the nut, the symptoms are a laboring motor and a slipping blade.

Arrows on lower blade guard (at bottom) and near center of blade, indicating direction of rotation, must agree when blade is installed.

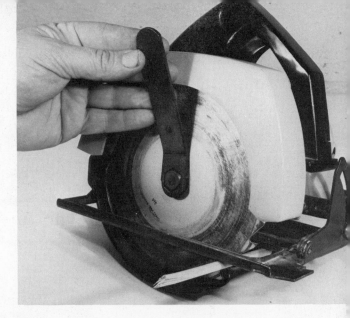

If saw has a slip clutch, blade must be tightened exactly according to manufacturer's instructions to avoid overloading the motor.

Before you start the job, take time to adjust the saw's blade depth. The blade cuts smoothest and safest when it protrudes about $^1/_4$ inch below the bottom of the work. Besides exposing least blade area, this allows the teeth to enter and leave the work at a shallow angle for least splintering. If you want to be a purist about this adjustment, estimate the height of a single tooth, then lower the blade to project at that length below the work. This technique is recommended for conventional steel teeth; for carbide-tipped blades, allow only a *half* tooth below the work to keep friction low for fast, cool cutting.

There may be no "good," or finished, side in construction timber, but a panel or plywood usually has a better surface on one side. To cause the least splintering on the good side, face it down before applying the saw. The teeth will enter the good side first, press it up against the tool's baseplate, then exit on the top side. It's on the exit (or "up") side that teeth tend to break an edge into splinters.

Spend a few moments providing good support for the work before sawing, and you'll be repaid for the effort. Either block the material above the floor or place it across sawhorses or other supports. Because a circular saw cuts so rapidly, check the right-of-way along the cutting route in advance; many a home craftsman has unwittingly sawed the material—plus a chair seat or something else concealed below the work! It also helps to plan the cut so the waste piece

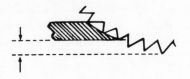

Adjust blade to depth of a full tooth below the work.

Proper positioning of saw on work. Heavy motor rests on good side of cut; waste side will fall off when it is cut through.

will fall off to your right as you face the work. This puts the full weight of the saw on the best-supported section of the work.

Next apply the blade to a guideline drawn on the work. Since the blade has thickness, you'll want to locate the blade on the waste side of the guideline to obtain an exact width. A bit of experimenting with scrap wood can quickly confer this skill—but chances are that if the waste piece will fall to your right, then you'll place the left (or inner) edge of the blade on the line. This puts the kerf in the waste side. After applying the blade, back off slightly, start the saw, and begin cutting as the blade reaches full speed. Use light pressure and don't force the tool, to avoid overheating. If you must stop before reaching the end of the line, release the trigger and allow the blade to come to complete rest before pulling the saw from the work. A coasting blade has enough residual force to snag and mar the work or to pull the saw out of your hands.

If you hit a damp or knotty section, don't force your way through or there'll be overheating and rough edges. Reduce forward pressure and allow the blade to work slowly through the area. Slow down, too, if you're cross-cutting against the grain and the wood shows signs of tearing.

Note that kerf, or cut, has significant width. Allow for it by applying blade to waste side of the work. In this case, blade is applied at right of the desired edge so that kerf falls in waste side (at right).

A circular saw's tendency to cut along a straight line is a boon to anyone's workmanship—but not if the saw strays from the line. After a bad start, don't force the blade back to the line but withdraw the saw and start again. With some experience you'll become adept at applying subtle pressures to make the blade track the line.

Routine cutting of small pieces can be done by eye, but long cuts in wide or narrow material call for some form of mechanical guidance. For accurate narrow cuts, install a rip guide on the saw and adjust it to the desired width. When the cut falls beyond the reach of the rip guide, tack or clamp a straight-edge on the work to serve as a reference. For speed and precision, always cut large panels with a straightedge guide, which may be a length of molding, metal shelf standard, or other straight piece.

Like the saber saw, a circular saw can make plunge (or pocket) cuts inside a panel without starting from the edge. Mark the area to be cut with guidelines and place the front edge of the saw base near one corner. Tilt the saw forward on edge until the blade is poised above the material. Then expose the blade by retracting the blade guard lever. With fingers well clear, start the motor and slowly tilt the saw backward until the blade lowers into the work. Now you can advance the saw up to the corner. To cut the remainder of the line, do not back up; lift the saw out of the work and turn it around. The remaining three sides of the cut-out area are done the same way.

To make an angle, or bevel, cut in the material, loosen the wing nut (or other control) to tilt the base the desired number of degrees, using the scale indicator (calibrated from 0 to 45 degrees) as a reference.

When sawing a large piece, a straightedge is clamped to work to guide saw.

Bevel cuts are obtained by tilting and locking saw at any angle on scale (lower right) between 0 and 45 degrees.

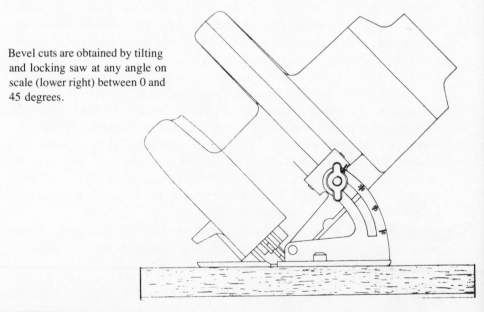

MAINTAINING THE CIRCULAR SAW

The most critical maintenance performed on a circular saw is at the lower blade guard, which unsheathes the blade as the saw advances on the work. Sawdust accumulates in the retracting mechanism and causes sticking. Unless the guard instantly snaps over the blade, damage may be caused if you pull the tool from the work and place it on a surface while the blade is still coasting. You may put the saw down and see it dance about the floor on the turning teeth. To avoid the dangerous consequences of sticking, check frequently to see that the guard snaps shut quickly and smoothly. Eliminate any rubbing or binding in the track by removing the blade and cleaning the interior with alcohol or kerosene. Cleanliness alone should take care of the problem; some manufacturers suggest that no lubrication be applied to the guard, the retracting spring, or its structure because grease or oil could encourage sawdust to stick in the mechanism.

Keep blades clean and sharp to reduce friction and possible kickback. Wood cutting deposits rosin (gum) on the blade, which lowers the cutting efficiency; remove it with hot water or kerosene. You can try your hand at

Lower blade guard must be kept free from binding by removing blade and clearing out sawdust. A sticking guard is hazardous.

touching up slightly worn blades with a file, following the original bevels, but a worn-out, dull blade should be treated by a professional. It's an excellent idea to have spare blades on hand to replace dull blades sent out for resharpening.

Bearings and carbon brushes in circular saws last many hours without attention. About every 20 hours the rear bearing should be lubricated with a few drops of SAE No. 20 oil if an access hole is provided in the motor housing. Front bearings and gears are lubricated by grease retained in the gear box. If there's any doubt about lubrication, follow the instruction manual. Some manuals say grease repacking is necessary whenever the brushes are replaced; the instructions may specify that the job should be done only by a service center.

The brushes in most circular saws are easily accessible for inspection by the owner, so check them occasionally to see that they have not worn to $1/4$ inch or less. Another item that wears out is the on-off switch. You'll extend its useful life by years if you never turn the saw on or off while the blade is pressed against a load. This precaution keeps heavy current surges from searing the switch contacts.

5

SANDER

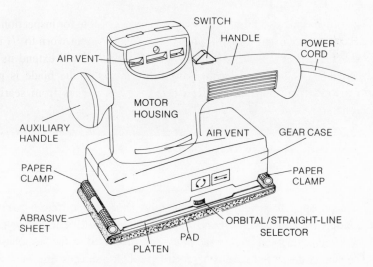

The tedious task of hand sanding with abrasive paper wrapped around a block accounts for the popularity of the electrified sander. It does the work five or six times faster. If you want to prepare a surface for refinishing, the sander turns drudgery into pleasure. You merely guide the tool over the course.

And a sander does much more. With the right abrasive it removes rust and old paint, polishes marble, cleans used lumber, or puts a beautiful surface on old wood for new projects. If you make a pencil mark at the wrong place on fresh, clean lumber, the sander erases it many times faster than you can by hand.

The power sander with the widest appeal goes under a variety of names— "finishing," "pad," "orbital," "straight-line," or "dual-action"—but you can quickly spot the general type by looking at the base, where you'll see a

Sander prepares an old surface for refinishing.

band of sandpaper stretched on a rectangular shoe. It's different from other basic sanders, which have a round disk or endless belt. These heavier-duty machines, more practical to rent than buy, are discussed in the last chapter.

The sander described here is a versatile tool. It produces fine finishes and, with coarse papers, does rough sanding as well. The latter job takes longer than with a heavy-duty sander, but a finishing sander should satisfy most needs in the home workshop. For tough, heavy-duty jobs like preparing a house exterior for painting, or auto body work, use a disk or belt sander.

THE BASIC SANDER

Housed atop a typical sander is a motor with its shaft pointing down. In some models the shaft engages an eccentric wheel to convert motor rotation into back-and-forth action. Vibration is reduced by a counterweight on the eccentric wheel. As the wheel generates reciprocating movement, it drives the rectangular platen, or base. In another design the motor spins a wheel that is weighted on one side to actuate the platen. Mounted on four rubber posts, the platen oscillates over an exceedingly short path—about $3/16$ inch.

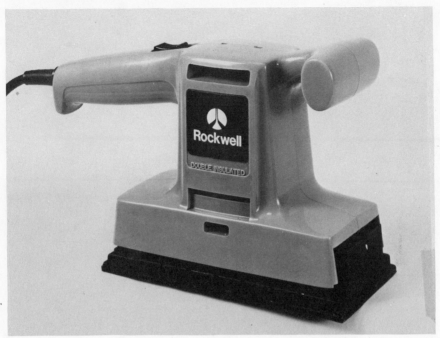

Motor, encased in vertical section, is cooled by air vents at top and bottom of housing.

A rubber socket on platen is vibrated by an off-balance wheel (visible in housing at left) to drive platen.

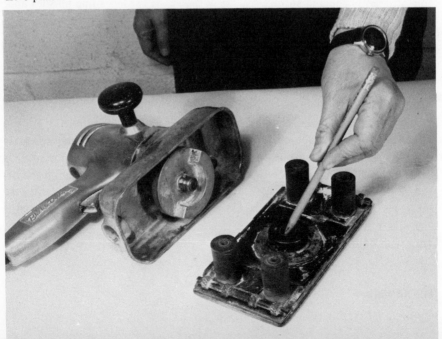

Switch selects either orbital or straight-line action.

If the platen moves with simple reciprocal motion, the tool is a *straight-line* sander. A platen may, however, follow a swirling, or *orbital,* path. Some models are *dual-action* sanders: they have a switch to choose either motion. Controlled by a motor of $^1/_5$ to $^1/_2$ hp, platen speed ranges from 4,000 to 10,000 strokes or orbits per minute to vibrate the abrasive sheet clamped around the ends of the platen. A rubber or neoprene pad acts as a leveling cushion between platen and sheet.

CHOOSING A SANDER

A hobbyist rarely needs a heavy-duty finishing sander for household projects. You can spot these models because of their high motor horsepower (about $^1/_2$ hp) and paper size of $4^1/_2$ by 11 inches. A light-duty machine will likely have only a $^1/_5$-hp motor and a paper size of $3^2/_3$ by 9 inches. Although papers come in precut pieces to fit a machine, you can also make your own from a standard 9- by 11-inch abrasive sheet. For installation in a heavy-duty machine the sheet is cut in half; for light-duty models the sheet is divided into three equal parts. Another difference between models is the dust collector. A large machine often has a built-in system for trapping sawdust—an optional accessory with lighter models.

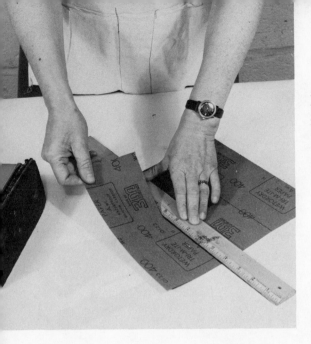

A standard abrasive sheet may be torn to measure and fitted to the machine.

At the least-expensive end of the spectrum is a very light-duty sander without a conventional motor. It's powered by a simple magnetically operated vibrator. In addition to the attraction of low cost, it has neither bearings nor brushes to wear out. These advantages are offset, however, by a limited ability to remove stock, so consider a vibrator sander only for the lightest finishing work. It can't do rough sanding and is neither as versatile nor as fast as a motor-driven model.

Another feature to consider in choosing a machine is type of sanding action: straight-line or orbital. There are a variety of models in each category, but the trend is to a tool with a selector that can do both. Straight-line sanding is

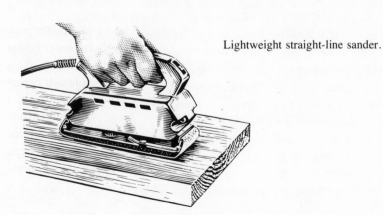

Lightweight straight-line sander.

A high-speed orbital sander produces the least cross-grain scratching. This model can operate at 10,000 orbits per minute.

essential for the finest finishing work. As platen and abrasive paper move back and forth, guided along the grain of the wood, you'll get the smoothest result—there is no cross-grain scratching to persist in the final finish. A disadvantage of straight-line operation is that it takes more time than does sanding across the grain. Orbital motion, on the other hand, does a bit of both—along and across the grain—and stock removal is faster. How fine the finish will be with orbital sanding depends on speed and stroke: machines with the highest speed and shortest strokes create the least visible scratching.

When choosing a model, grip the sander and see if it's comfortable to move over the surface. An auxiliary handle makes the machine easier to guide and support on vertical surfaces like a wall or when raised to the ceiling. That handle becomes increasingly important if the tool's weight is more than about 5

Auxiliary handle improves control of a heavy sander.

pounds. If you are permitted to operate the sander before buying it, see if you can easily control its direction. Feel for excessive vibration, which is annoying on long jobs. Can you conveniently reach the on-off switch? Some switches can be locked on to relieve steady finger pressure on the trigger.

Also inspect the hardware that holds the abrasive paper to the platen. Some models have a roller arrangement that draws in the paper ends under tension. Others have a clamp that grips the paper ends. Whatever the system, paper changing should be a simple job with a wrench or screwdriver. Check too whether the tool has any side projections beyond the sanding area; they could prevent the machine from reaching into tight corners and close to vertical obstructions.

Finally, determine if brush replacement is done without disassembling most of the housing. Double insulation, offered in some models, reduces shock hazard and eliminates a 3-wire cord.

ABRASIVE PAPERS

Inexpensive flint paper for hand sanding isn't durable enough in a motor-driven tool. Garnet or aluminum oxide paper is a much better choice. To save

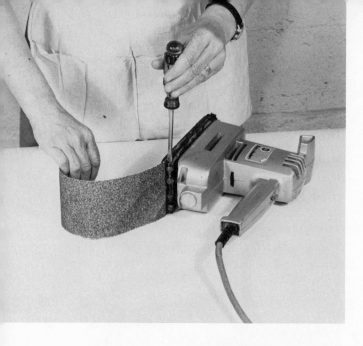

End clamp is turned by screw-driver to install paper.

Compact design of this sander allows it to be maneuvered very close to adjacent obstructions.

some expense you can obtain standard-size sheets and divide them in halves or thirds to fit the machine. Tear them against a straightedge, not free-hand; you'll need a neat edge for a good grip by the rollers or clamp.

You'll want an assortment of papers with different degrees of abrasive power, according to grit size. Papers are described by the general terms "coarse," for rough wood sanding; "medium," for general wood sanding; and "fine," for smoothing wood or plaster. "Extra-fine" does final sanding of bare wood or smoothing of old paint. If you purchase a basic assortment of precut aluminum oxide papers, it may include the following grit sizes: No. 150, No. 120, No. 100, and No. 80 (fine); No. 60 and No. 50 (medium); and No. 40 (coarse). It's advisable to move up this scale of abrasiveness one or two steps at a time—from coarse to fine—to achieve a smooth, scratch-free finish.

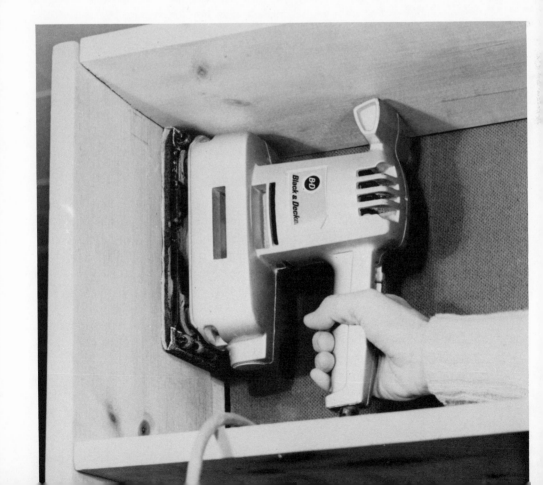

DUST COLLECTOR

A dust-collecting attachment provides cleaner room air, results in less mess to sweep after sanding, and helps to keep the paper from clogging. The attachment for a typical sander consists of an apron that fits around the platen area and a standard hose connection to a vacuum cleaner. On large machines the built-in dust collector has its own dust bag. Remember that if you use a vacuum cleaner, you'll have to tote the hose along with the sander when you move about a large area.

HOW TO USE A SANDER

Before you place the sander on the work, turn on the power. When the pad is flat against the work, begin to move the sander in long, overlapping strokes with the grain. This provides the smoothest results. Work slowly, but never allow the tool to dwell in one spot or it may bite into the surface. Keep up a continuous motion until you're finished; then stop the motor, *after* you lift the sander from the work.

Do not press down while sanding. The only force needed is the weight of the tool itself; the abrasive paper does the work. Too much pressure quickly wears the paper, reduces motor speed, and mars the work. As the sander approaches an obstruction, watch out not to let the machine strike and scratch it.

A general technique to obtain a smooth finish on bare wood is to start with a paper that's just coarse enough to remove ridges, high spots, and surface roughness—No. 60 or 80 paper, for example. Always move with the grain. Then, to further improve the surface, change to a No. 80 or 100 paper. Continue the progression with a No. 100 or 120 paper, and end with a still finer abrasive—say, No. 120 or 150—if you need a high degree of smoothness. A sleek, fine-furniture appearance is possible with a No. 220 paper, followed by polishing with a length of lamb's wool clipped to the pad. One secret of obtaining a good finish: don't change from coarse to fine paper in a single step. It will almost certainly cause swirl marks in the work. Use small increments of only one or two grit grades at a time.

Orbital action, that is, simultaneously cutting with and across the grain, removes material faster than straight-line sanding. Use it for sanding down patches made of epoxy, fiberglass, and metal-base solder. Old paint and varnish come off with orbital action using a coarse, open-coat No. 40 paper.

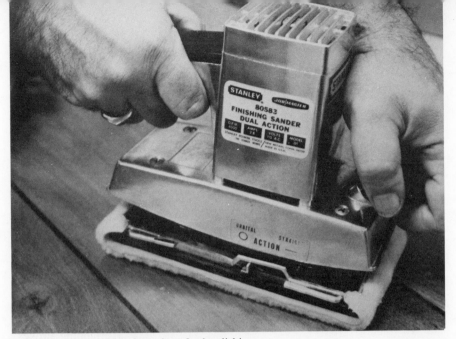

Lamb's wool secured to base does final polishing.

Unlike wood, which chars when friction is excessive, paint and similar substances soften when heated. Avoid this condition by using wide strokes so as not to concentrate the sander's action in a small area. Occasionally examine the paper to see if it's clogged with melted material; renew the abrasive if necessary.

Sanding is an excellent way to handle one notorious job that plagues many amateurs: smoothing newly dried plaster applied over a taped joint in wallboard or sheet rock. With a fine-grit, open-coat abrasive, the sander evenly reduces excess plaster to the level of the adjacent wall surface. Use circular, overlapping movements and sweep a large area. One pitfall to avoid is digging the side of the paper into the plaster—take care to keep the sanding pad level as you sweep. After the high spots are leveled, use broad strokes to feather the edges of the plaster until it merges with the rest of the wall. Much plaster dust is generated during the job, so clean the machine after you're done to prevent unreasonable wear in the motor and bearings.

MAINTAINING THE SANDER

Because a sander generates fine particles as it works, it soon becomes coated and clogged with dust. Professionals use compressed air to blow out foreign matter, but at home use a soft brush or a rubber bulb to keep the tool

RECOMMENDED ABRASIVE SHEETS

Material to Be Sanded	For Material Removal		For Regular Finish		For Fine Finish	
	Type of Abrasive	Grit No.	Type of Abrasive	Grit No.	Type of Abrasive	Grit No.
Softwood; Soft wallboard	Cabinet paper (garnet)	2–1	Cabinet paper (garnet)	1/2–2/0	Finishing paper (garnet)	3/0–5/0
Plastic	Cabinet paper (aluminum oxide)	60–100	Wet paper—C weight (silicon carbide)	120–220	Wet paper—A weight (silicon carbide)	240–600
Hardwood; Hard composition wallboard	Cabinet paper (aluminum oxide)	36–50	Cabinet paper (aluminum oxide)	60–100	Finishing paper (aluminum oxide)	120–180
Soft metal	Metal-working cloth (aluminum oxide)	36–60	Cabinet paper (aluminum oxide)	80–120	Wet paper (silicon carbide)	150–320
Hard metal	Metal-working cloth (aluminum oxide)	40–60	Metal-working cloth (aluminum oxide)	80–120	Metal-working cloth in oil (aluminum oxide)	150–320 or crocus
Hard, brittle minerals and compositions	Cabinet paper (aluminum oxide)	50–80	Finishing paper (aluminum oxide)	100–180	Wet paper—A weight (silicon carbide)	220–320
Hard, tough minerals and composition	Metal-working cloth (aluminum oxide)		Metal-working cloth (aluminum oxide)	80–120	Finishing paper (aluminum oxide)	150–320
Paint and varnish	Cabinet paper (open-coat garnet)	2 1/2–1 1/2			Wet paper—A weight (silicon carbide)	240–400

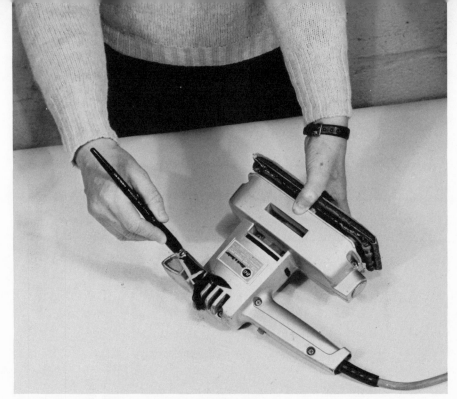

Air vents must be kept clear to prevent overheating.

clean. Some sanders have a rear armature bearing near the commutator that occasionally needs a few drops of light machine oil injected through a hole in the housing.

The gear case also needs periodic attention. With the plug removed from the outlet, disassemble the platen and counterweight, and regrease the transmission chamber with lubricant recommended by the manufacturer. His instructions should also give any special details about how to inspect and replace motor brushes.

6

SOLDERING IRON AND PROPANE TORCH

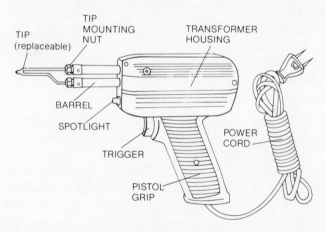

TIP
(replaceable)

TIP
MOUNTING
NUT

TRANSFORMER
HOUSING

BARREL

SPOTLIGHT

TRIGGER

POWER
CORD

PISTOL
GRIP

A slug of copper on a long handle thrust into a flame was the standard soldering tool until a few decades ago. Today's equivalent, powered by gas or electricity, is both useful and convenient. Although there are a bewildering number of models, soldering irons are among the most inexpensive tools you can buy for the workshop. It's not impractical to buy more than one type and be ready for any possibility from an earring repair to a major plumbing installation.

Consider the electrically powered soldering iron. In smaller sizes it's the essential tool for electronic work, such as wiring kits, and for repairing and splicing appliance and house wiring. Specially shaped accessories equip it for such craft work as wood burning, leather tooling, and plastic sculpture. Irons of moderate power handle sheet metal work, while big brutes cope with gutters and downspouts.

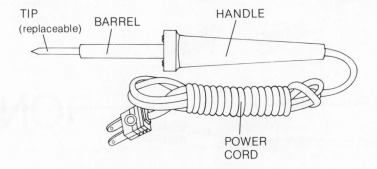

TIP
(replaceable)　BARREL　　　　HANDLE

POWER
CORD

BASIC SOLDERING IRONS

Soldering is not the same as gluing. It is a fusion of metals into an alloy that occurs only in a narrow heat range. If the solder and the work fail to form an alloy because of insufficient heat, the result is a weak, powdery "cold-solder joint." The connection will suffer poor mechanical strength and low electrical conductivity. Too much heat, on the other hand, ruins the job because the essential cleaning agent, flux, oxidizes and loses effectiveness.

To generate the right amount of heat and deliver it to the correct point, iron manufacturers offer three basic designs. One of the most familiar is the *soldering gun,* so called because of a pistol-like appearance and trigger switch. The idea of the gun is to generate heat with almost no warm-up delay. This is usually accomplished by a massive step-down transformer which reduces 120-volt house current to a few volts while feeding it to a looping "hairpin" that forms the tip of the iron. The step-down action sends a huge current through

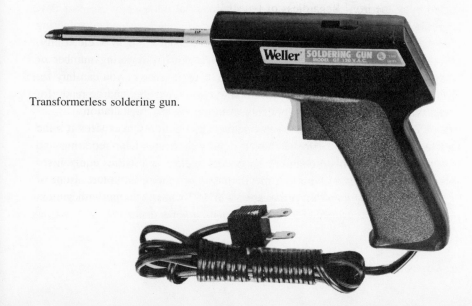

Transformerless soldering gun.

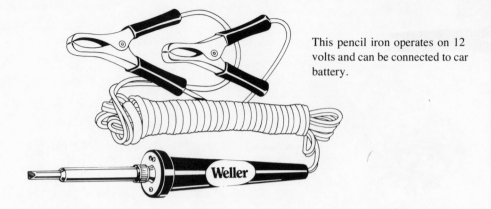

This pencil iron operates on 12 volts and can be connected to car battery.

the tip to generate rapid heating at a safe voltage. The bare tip presents no electrical hazard.

A more recent series of guns are *transformerless*. The circuit, equipped with built-in temperature regulation, sends a large inrush of current to heat the tip rapidly, then reduces temperature to desired operating level. These guns can be recognized by a single tube emerging from the end instead of a hairpin loop.

Pencil irons are another category. Mostly small in dimension, they contain a heating element that takes several minutes to reach operating temperature. The small size and light weight of a pencil iron make it valuable for delicate work. Although most irons plug into house current, there are 12-volt models that can operate from a car battery for outdoor work.

CHOOSING AN IRON

Begin with wattage rating, which tells the amount of electrical power consumed by the iron. Regardless of type, all irons fall into one or more of three approximate categories.

A *light-duty* iron has a range extending from about 10 to 50 watts. Almost all radio, TV, and other electronic work (such as kit building) is done at these wattages. A 10-watter can touch tiny printed-circuit wiring without scorching electronic parts. An iron in the 20- to 50-watt class is excellent for general electronic wiring, as attaching components to terminals and lugs. An iron in this category can also solder small jewelry items. The light-duty iron will not be effective on a large mass of metal, which rapidly dissipates heat and lowers the iron's temperature. This problem rarely occurs in electronic work unless you're soldering a thick ground wire to a metal chassis or joining large metal pieces.

Ratings for *medium-duty* irons are 50 to 150 watts. This is the best compromise for the occasional solderer who wants a general purpose tool. At this

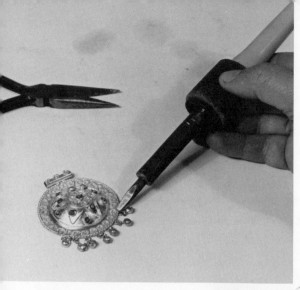

A 40-watt pencil with chisel tip is an excellent general-purpose iron for wiring and other small work.

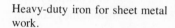

Heavy-duty iron for sheet metal work.

power you can splice and solder the heavy No. 14 and No. 12 solid copper wires found in household wiring and appliances. There's sufficient heat, too, to repair small metal toys and other items fabricated of light sheet metal.

A *heavy-duty* iron, at a wattage of 150 or above, is rarely used in the home. It's more suited to tradesmen who work with large or thick metal pieces. Don't consider it for plumbing, where soldering is done on copper pipes and fittings, because a propane torch is vastly more effective.

In addition to wattage, an iron's specifications may quote "tip temperature." This rating, however, is to assist engineers in choosing specialized irons for commercial production work. For example, a tip for delicate electronic work is rated at about 600 degrees; heavier electrical work requires about 800 degrees.

The wattage categories are not rigid. If you purchase a medium-duty iron of 100 watts or so, you can also solder a thin wire or component with it by applying heat for a short duration. For frequent light-duty work, however, you'll want a smaller iron because it's physically easier to wield near delicate parts. That raises the next important consideration: whether to solder with an iron or a gun.

The casual solderer is often attracted by the soldering gun because it remains cool until the trigger is squeezed. A gun lends itself to intermittent operation and is especially convenient when you're working away from bench or table. Standard transformer-type guns are sold in medium- and heavy-duty models with wattages that start at about 100 and rise to about 300. Guns are also made with dual-capacity wattage ratings, in these typical combinations: 100/145, 145/210, and 240/325. Low or high wattage is selected by an appropriate squeeze on the trigger.

More flexibility is possible with the newer single-tube guns. By interchanging tubes you can obtain two heat ranges—25 to 100 watts, and 100 to 200 watts; or you can acquire a three-range model that adds a 200-to-450-watt level. Thus you can tailor the tool to almost any job. Another advantage of a single-tube gun is a narrow tip. You can manipulate it with great dexterity in tight corners.

If you're an electronic hobbyist or enjoy sitting at a workbench for lengthy sessions, don't choose a gun as your primary soldering instrument. A stereo

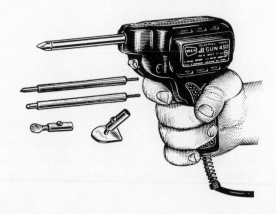

Single-tube gun with interchangeable tips.

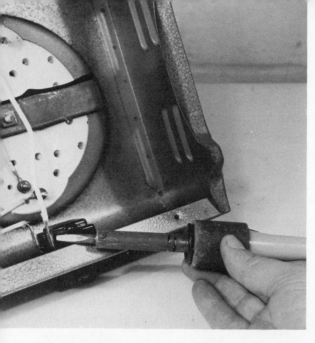

A pencil iron is adept at soldering inside a chassis.

receiver or color TV can have a thousand solder joints, and guns are too un-wieldy to grasp, lift, and squeeze dozens of times each hour. For work of this sort a pencil iron is more suitable. Weighing only ounces, it has excellent bal-ance and a slender tip that moves easily about the tangle of wires and small parts in a chassis. Interchangeable heating elements in some models allow the pencil iron to produce a number of tip temperatures or accept a variety of dif-ferent tips. For electronic work, choose a working wattage of about 25 to 50 watts and a chisel-type tip. For very fine work on integrated circuits and micro-miniature components (such as a radio control rig for a model airplane), a 10-watter forestalls any threat of danger. The disadvantages of a pencil iron—warm-up time is several minutes, and the iron remains hot as long as the plug is in the outlet—are not significant in bench work.

Some pencil models feature interchangeable tips for varying wattage rating.

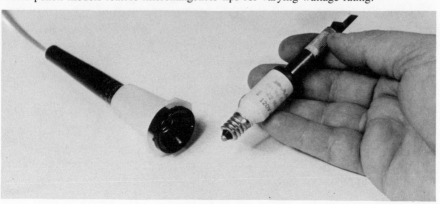

The old-fashioned soldering iron with heavy copper tip is best reserved for metal work. Wattages run from about 170 to more than 500. When soldering flat surfaces, as with sheet metal, the tip of a standard iron is far more effective than the narrow "hairpin" of a gun, even though the wattage rating may be the same for both. The broad surface of the iron's chisel tip efficiently applies heat directly to the work. With a fine tip, heat is quickly conducted away from the joint by the surrounding metal.

COMPONENTS AND MATERIALS

After your iron, the most important item you'll buy is solder. Its make-up is expressed as a ratio of tin to lead; for example, 60-40 solder means 60 per-cent tin, 40 percent lead. The more tin, the better the solder bond—and the higher the price. Electrical and electronic work is done with 60-40 solder. When working with metal, however, you may use a 40-60 mixture. Lead is a potentially poisonous substance, so any project that will be used for food or drinking water should be soldered with a special tin-*silver* compound made for the purpose.

Once you've selected a solder formula, consider the flux. A chemical agent, flux cleans the joint to counteract the oxidizing effect of the iron's heat. In some solders the flux is stored in a hollow core and is automatically released to the joint as the solder melts. A solder core may contain either of two flux types, and it's important to know the difference.

Acid flux is solely for metal work—sheet metal projects, repairing metal items, and the like. Never use acid flux or acid-core solder on electrical wiring or electronic parts; its corrosive action creates electrical resistance in the joint, which could cause a circuit malfunction many months later. Kit manufacturers will void the guarantee on an electronic project that's assembled with acid-core solder.

Electronic and electrical wiring are soldered with *rosin* flux. One device for remembering which flux is used for which type of work is: "*r*osin for *r*adio." In nearly all instances a rosin-core solder of 60-40 composition is a good choice for electrical work.

Wire solder is solid and has no flux. It commonly joins, or "sweats," cop-per plumbing fittings and sheet metal with the aid of an acid flux in paste or liquid form applied to the joint.

Soldering tips come in a variety of types. Most soldering is done using the *chisel* tip, but other specialized shapes cut plastic and asphalt tile, burn patterns

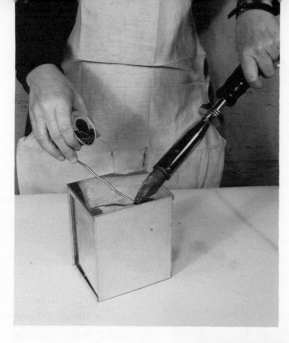

A heavy-duty, high-wattage iron
is needed for soldering large
metal pieces.

Acid and rosin soldering flux.

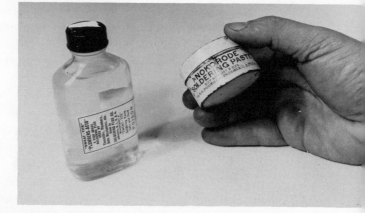

Rosin-core solder (at left) is for
electrical work. Solid wire solder
is ideal for plumbing.

Specially shaped tip can be used in a pencil iron to cut plastic.

in wood, remove putty, seal plastic bags, and remove dents and scratches from furniture. Try to select a tip that places the greatest possible amount of heating surface against the work. An exception is printed-circuit boards, where a cone-shaped tip is used to keep the iron from spreading heat beyond the point of soldering.

To work in close quarters, a *soldering-aid tool* is of interest. It's a slim shaft with a notch on one end and a point on the other. Because the tool is of aluminum (which won't attract solder without a special flux) it can wiggle free connections that are embedded in molten solder. Another accessory to remove connections is a *desoldering tool*. It is a rubber bulb with a Teflon tip (which won't melt) that is applied to the heated joint. By squeezing, then releasing, the bulb, you can draw (or "sip") liquid solder into it. A *solder wick* is still another desoldering aid, that works by capillary action. Placed on the hot joint, the wick draws the solder into a myriad of tiny spaces.

Many soldering irons come with a bent-wire stand that holds the hot tip above the work surface. The stand is easily knocked over, however, if you reach across the table, as the scorches on your forearms will soon prove. The trouble with a wire stand is that the iron remains exposed. Far more practical is a cage-like stand that completely encircles the iron as it supports it.

There is little burn hazard with a soldering gun because the tip cools quickly. But there is another annoying problem: If your work area is cluttered, which is hardly unusual, there is no place to put down the gun except near the table edge. A brush of your arm inevitably pushes the gun off the edge, and the plastic case may shatter on the floor. The high-impact-resistance plastics used for so many other products have somehow eluded the soldering-gun industry.

Desoldering tools. Rubber bulb "sips" molten solder to remove connections.

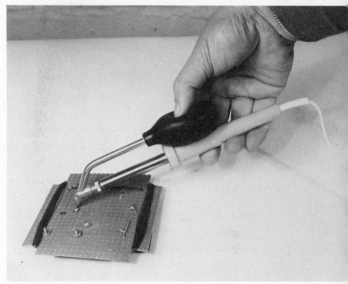

Cage-type stand affords good protection from soldering iron.

After damaging three guns this way, I finally solved the problem with two L-shaped brackets fastened to the workbench to form a holster for the gun whenever it is put down.

HOW TO USE AN IRON

"Ninety percent of all defective kits are repaired by resoldering every joint." Those were the words of an engineer and major kit maker when asked what went wrong when people built electronic kits. Factory troubleshooters, he explained, merely apply a hot iron to correct faulty connections, cold-solder joints, and other products of poor soldering technique. The builders' problem springs from a widespread misbelief that solder should be heated until it melts and runs onto the parts. Such a joint may look good, but the solder often fails to form a durable alloy intrinsically. The error is avoided by following a single rule: the iron must initially heat the *work*—the wire, terminal, metal piece, pipe, or other item to be soldered. The work in turn heats the solder. Now molten solder runs onto surfaces that are sufficiently hot to form an alloy.

Work with a well-tinned iron. To prepare for tinning, clean a pitted, oxidized tip while it is cool with fine sandpaper or steel wool. Heat the tip and apply a liberal coat of solder, wait a minute, then wipe the tip clean with a damp rag or sponge. It should leave the tip clean and shiny.

The work should be clean too. In electrical work, wires and terminals are usually clean and dirt isn't a major problem. Sheet metal, however, may need cleaning with a wire brush or sandpaper to get rid of dirt or corrosion.

Always use gentle pressure in laying the iron's broadest surface on the joint—where parts or wires meet. When the area is sufficiently hot, apply the solder. How do you know when solder is ready to form an alloy? That's simple; the solder furnishes the signal. By holding the solder against the joint as you apply heat, you can see the solder start to melt. Allow a small amount of solder to run into the joint to form a *thin* covering. Remove the iron, then remain absolutely still until the solder "freezes." Any disturbance of the work during the cooling period almost guarantees a crumbly, cold-solder connection. Signs of a good solder joint are a bright, shiny finish (not dull gray) and a faint outline of parts or wires embedded in the solder. A ribbed appearance means the solder has truly penetrated the connection.

Skilled workers often use a slightly modified technique with large areas that draw away the iron's heat and prevent good thermal build-up. As the iron is held to the work, solder is fed to the tip until a small pool forms between the

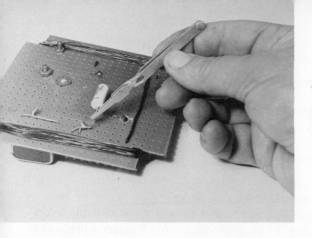

Tweezers-like heat sink clips to lead of small electronic part (white tube) to absorb heat when connection is soldered.

tip and the joint. It creates a heat reservoir that quickly concentrates high temperature at the desired spot.

Overheating is a danger if the iron is not removed after solder flows. Excess heat damages components or oxidizes and weakens the joint. When soldering tiny components that can't take much heat, use a heat *sink*. Almost any metal implement can be a sink—an alligator clip, the tips of pliers—if it grips the wire between the part and the iron to block heat flow to the delicate area. If you do much electronic work, buy a handy pincer-like heat sink ready-made for the job.

MAINTAINING AN IRON

Besides keeping a tip tinned, smooth it occasionally with a fine file. Copper tips are easiest to restore because they're solid and you can safely remove some surface material to renew them. Some tips, though, have a thin plating that won't stand up under much abrasive action.

Soldering guns suffer a heat loss after a few months, but it's almost always due to loosening of the nuts that hold the tip. After a number of heating cycles, the nuts relax or corrosion creeps into them. Since tip connections must function at extremely low electrical resistance, occasionally retighten the mounting hardware. If this doesn't help, remove the tip and make sure its contact surfaces are clean.

Soldering irons and pencils with replaceable tips or heating elements are subject to the same problem, so check their mountings occasionally for security. The small tips on pencils often corrode and lock in place. You can avoid this difficulty by coating the tip threads with graphite or the special lubricant sold by iron manufacturers.

THE BASIC PROPANE TORCH

None of the instruments just described delivers the intense heat needed for some jobs around the home—such as "sweating" copper pipes and fittings for household plumbing jobs. Other high-heat work includes bending metal, thawing pipes, and softening paint. All these tasks are efficiently done with a propane torch. Safer than a gasoline blowtorch, a propane torch is easy to operate and completely portable, meaning you don't need an extension cord.

A typical torch has a cylindrical fuel tank containing about 27 fluid ounces of liquid propane under pressure. A check valve at the top ensures that fuel will not escape, even if the burner is unscrewed. Inside the burner are a needle valve for controlling gas flow, a filter to remove impurities, and intake ports to draw in outside air to support a flame of nearly 3000 degrees F. When the control knob is turned the valve releases pressurized propane, which expands several hundred times in turning from a liquid into a gas.

There is little difference between propane torches of various manufacture, but improvements are occasionally seen. The most annoying problem with a torch is a tendency for the flame to change in length as the torch is tilted. This characteristic, caused by inability of the regulator to control the fuel flow, can be dangerous when soldering in a tight corner with the burner inverted. The sound of the flame changes abruptly from a whisper to a roar! It takes some juggling to get the right valve setting for a particular angle. For the same

Propane torch. Knob being turned controls valve to regulate gas flow and length of flame.

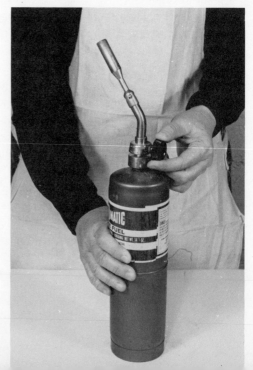

reason, when the torch points nearly straight down it may sputter or flame out completely as liquid propane inside the tank sloshes over the feed valve.

Late-model torches have overcome these deficiencies. Improved regulators control the liquid gas regardless of how you hold the tank. Another welcome feature eliminates the nuisance of relighting the torch. Older models required repeated trials with a match or flint and different control settings before the flame burned steadily. At least one manufacturer now offers a built-in pilot light. Press a lever on the burner head, and a tiny flame bursts into full length. This feature permits you to extinguish the flame when not in use, which is safer because you may tip over a lighted torch left on the floor while you tend to other phases of the job. The hot flame could quickly ignite something. It's a good idea to keep water handy to douse any fire, especially while soldering in a wall or a tight corner.

ACCESSORIES

You can buy a propane torch in a kit with a dozen or so accessories, or purchase it as a basic unit and add what you need. The torch can be supplied with a *utility burner,* an all-purpose hollow tube for sweat-soldering copper fittings, thawing frozen pipes, and most general work. A wide-mouth attachment called a *flame spreader* fits over the basic burner to fan the flame over a wide area. For heavy-duty metal work purchase a *soldering tip,* a massive chisel-like tip heated by the gas flame. A *pencil burner* attachment squeezes the flame into a point to confine heat in a narrow area for precision work. Another useful accessory is a *spark lighter,* which ignites the torch more conveniently than does a match.

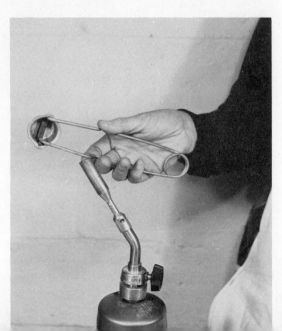

Spark lighter—flint rubbing against a steel rasp—ignites torch much more easily than does a match.

HOW TO USE A PROPANE TORCH

There's a knack to soldering with a propane torch, so try your hand first on scrap pieces. To develop sweat-soldering skill, start by cleaning a copper fitting with fine sandpaper, emery paper, or steel wool, and coat each mating surface with noncorrosive flux. Insert the pipe into the fitting and rotate it a few times to distribute flux throughout the joint. Move the torch to the joint and play the flame across the crack between fitting and pipe until the flux bubbles and the joint emits steam. Press the end of the wire solder into the joint. If temperature is sufficient, the solder moves rapidly into the joint and fills the internal gap through capillary action. It's not necessary to move the wire solder to fill the joint; keep feeding at the same point. When a ring of solder appears completely around the joint, quickly withdraw the torch. Overheating must be avoided or solder flows out of the joint, possibly causing a water leak later on.

Ends of copper pipe, where solder will flow, must be shiny.

Torch is aimed at crack where pipe enters fitting. Wire solder will be drawn into joint when the copper is sufficiently hot.

A good solder joint is ruined if it's jostled while still cooling. Wait about a minute before touching the joint or allowing water to flow through the pipe. Plumbers wipe a hot joint with a brush or rag to give it a shiny, neat appearance, but don't try it if there's any risk of disturbing the solder as it solidifies.

MAINTAINING THE PROPANE TORCH

A torch solders dozens of joints before requiring maintenance or other attention. The first sign to indicate a waning gas supply is a failing flame. This means it's time for a replacement cylinder; there's no need to purchase a whole new burner head. If the torch feeds intermittently, causing an unreliable flame, the opening in the burner head may be clogged. This is repaired by unscrewing the head and installing a replacement orifice available for purchase.

7

BENCH GRINDER AND HAND-HELD GRINDER

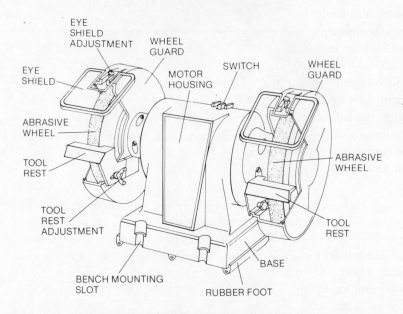

EYE
SHIELD
ADJUSTMENT

EYE
SHIELD

WHEEL
GUARD

MOTOR
HOUSING

SWITCH

WHEEL
GUARD

ABRASIVE
WHEEL

TOOL
REST

TOOL
REST
ADJUSTMENT

ABRASIVE
WHEEL

TOOL
REST

BASE

BENCH MOUNTING
SLOT

RUBBER FOOT

A bench grinder is a restorative instrument. It does many jobs around the shop, but keeping other tools sharp is the most important function. Acquire one and you'll discover the satisfaction and economic rewards of rescuing a blunt tool from the scrap heap. With careful technique a grinder can return a tool to factory condition. Sharp tools make work go faster with less marring and chopping of the material. Safety is improved too—a worn tool easily slips and causes injury.

No shop should be without a flat sharpening stone for honing tool edges by hand, but a bench grinder goes much further. When the stone no longer brings back a keen edge, the bench grinder has the power to reshape a tool's bevel to its original angle. You can restore the cutting edges of chisels, drill bits, punches, and reshape battered screwdriver tips. Replace the grinding wheel with a wire brush, and the tool cleans away rust—or, with a buffing wheel, polishes. We'll also look at a hand-held grinder, a more recent instrument that does exquisitely delicate craft work on small items and grinding jobs that are too fine for the bench type.

THE BASIC BENCH GRINDER

The heart of a bench grinder is an electric motor with shafts extending left and right to hold wheels and attachments. The drive is direct, with no gears or belts, at a horsepower rating of from $^1/_4$ to $^3/_4$ hp. To spin the abrasive wheels, 5 to 8 inches in diameter, the motor attains speeds of 3000 to 3600 rpm.

Several refinements on the housing protect the operator. The wheels are almost completely surrounded by guards to expose only a wheel's working area. Transparent eye shields cover most of the remaining surface to block sparks and flying debris. To give you a firm base for pressing the work against the grinder, a tool rest is mounted next to the rim of each wheel. Rubber feet on the bottom prevent "walking," and the base has predrilled holes so that you can permanently fasten the tool to the bench.

CHOOSING A BENCH GRINDER

The grinder's given size refers to wheel diameter. Heavy-duty models turn 8-inch wheels, while smaller grinders hold 5-, 6-, or 7-inch wheels. Horsepower also varies with wheel diameter. In an 8-inch model the motor may be rated at $^3/_4$ hp, while capacities of smaller grinders decrease to $^1/_4$ hp. Rarely will a home workshop require a heavy-duty grinder. A large model does offer certain advantages: since it presents a wider wheel area to the work, it does the job faster, and it is less prone to stalling if you bear hard on the wheel. Heavy-duty grinders, also, are fitted with ball bearings for long service. But a 5- or 6-inch grinder of moderate or low power should fulfill most people's needs at home. Besides costing less, the light-duty grinder occupies less room on the worktable.

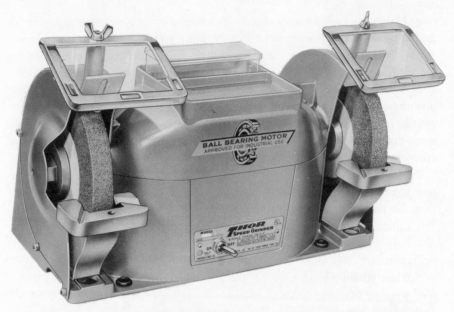

Slots in tool rests (in front of wheels) hold drill bits at correct angle for resharpening.

Look at the on-off switch to see if it's within ready reach. Examine the tool rests. They should be adjustable in two ways: distance from the grinding wheel and tilt. Unless the rest can be adjusted to lie close to the wheel, the work could jam in the opening. The tilting feature of the tool rest lets you grind a tool at any prescribed angle. Some rests have a formed slot that correctly holds a drill bit for sharpening.

Another desirable feature is an adjustable eye shield. With a large piece of work you might have to move the shield temporarily out of the way (and rely on goggles for eye protection). Still another handy feature is a water tray— you'll want to douse metal objects in water to prevent overheating. Some grinders have a built-in light to illuminate the work; or you may purchase one as an accessory.

ACCESSORIES

The grinder manufacturer provides a pair of general-purpose wheels that are suited to most grinding jobs in the workshop. For sharpening knives, drill bits, axes, and other wood-cutting tools, one wheel is probably 60-grit. A coarser, 36-grit companion on the other side tackles rough or fast grinding of most materials. To bolster this basic complement, consider a *carbide* wheel for grinding very hard items such as carbide-tipped tools. Other wheels are sold in various grit sizes to cope with work beyond routine grinding. A fine, 100-grit wheel, for example, is for keen-edge tools, finish grinding, and polishing.

A soft *buffing* wheel rounds out the assortment. To aid the buffing action you may purchase special compounds to enhance a specific finish—for example, red rouge for polishing gold, silver, and other precious metals; white rouge for nickel, chrome, iron, stainless steel, cast brass, and aluminum; or an emery compound for removing rust, scale, and tarnish.

The crisp edges of a new grinding wheel disintegrate in time under abrasive stresses. The rim also tends to glaze over, which reduces the grinding action. To restore a wheel to maximum performance, consider a *wheel dresser*. The cutters on this accessory keep the wheel smooth and true. A grinder should also have a pair of *wire wheel brushes,* in coarse and fine versions, for clean-up operations.

Most grinding jobs are done with the work held in the hand, but an *edge tool grinding attachment* improves your accuracy. This device holds the item—tool, blade, scissors, screwdriver, or garden implement—at the recommended angle and feeds it at a controlled rate. (If you buy this accessory, be sure it will fit your grinder model.) Another accessory is a *pedestal* to convert a bench grinder into a floor model. With prebored holes, the pedestal can bolt to the floor to keep the grinder stationary.

HOW TO USE A BENCH GRINDER

As you press the work against the spinning wheel, the grinder tends to "walk" across the table. Designers counter this with rubber strips and pre-drilled holes in the grinder base. It's strongly recommended that you securely fasten the grinder to the workbench with wood screws or machine bolts. Tighten the base enough to slightly squeeze the rubber feet; this allows the rubber to absorb vibration for quieter operation. On most grinding jobs adjust the tool rest to slightly below the wheel's center.

Before you start a grinder, beware of two hazards. The machine develops tremendous centrifugal force, and a defective wheel might shatter with dire consequences. (How to detect a bad wheel is explained on page 100.) A few sensible precautions diminish the danger. When you switch on the motor, don't stand in a direct line with a wheel until it spins at normal speed for a few moments. And don't grind on the side of a wheel unless the manufacturer advises it.

Grinder should be fastened to workbench to prevent "walking" when work is applied to wheel.

Another potential danger is that the work may be grabbed in the crack between the wheel and tool rest. Since the tool rest is usually adjustable, make certain that clearance is not more than about $\frac{1}{16}$ to $\frac{1}{8}$ inch. The clearance grows as the wheel wears down and must be occasionally checked.

If your grinder has a water tray, fill it before grinding metal. If there is no tray keep a supply of water nearby. Heat developed in metal quickly destroys a tool's temper and cutting edge, so quench the tool in water if there's any heat build-up. Lessening the feed pressure causes less heating but it also lengthens grinding time. Use your judgment to determine the right pressure, how long to hold the tool against the wheel during a pass, and when to immerse it in water.

It's unwise to grind a tool that is merely dull—you'll remove too much material. Chances are that touching up the tool with a stone will revive the cutting edge. Grind only when a completely new bevel (the slanting edge) is needed due to scoring, nicks, or scallops. In many instances you can do a good job without knowing the exact grinding angle if you carefully observe the original bevel ground by the manufacturer. Study the angle, then apply the bevel surface flat against the wheel. Move the bevel from side to side evenly across the rim of the wheel. After a few swipes check the edge for keenness to see whether you're following the original bevel angle.

Here are the recommended angles for several tools. The figures refer to the *included* angle—the one formed by either the centerline of the tool or its base

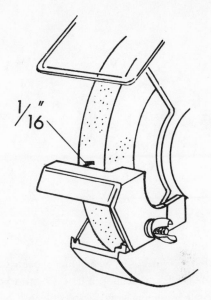

Tool rest should be no farther than ¹/₁₆ to ¹/₈ inch from wheel.

1/16″

with respect to the slant of the beveled edge. (For a pointed tool the angle is included between the slanting sides.) A wood chisel or plane blade, for example, is ground to approximately 25 degrees; a prick punch to 60 degrees; a center punch to 90 degrees; a cold chisel to 70 degrees. A screwdriver is ground to follow the original taper, and its end—the part that engages the screw—is squared off.

Don't expect a grinding wheel to do the *final* finishing. If a tool, such as a knife, needs a fine edge complete the job with an oiled sharpening stone. Honing by hand also removes small marks or burrs left by the grinding wheel.

MAINTAINING THE BENCH GRINDER

One item that deserves close attention is the tool rests. They will need occasional adjustment to keep them no more than ¹/₈ inch from the wheels. Use the wheel dresser to keep the wheels running true. There is no need to replace brushes because bench grinders generally have brushless induction motors. Lubrication, too, is rarely called for because bearings are sealed and impregnated with sufficient lubricant for the life of a grinder operated in the intermittent pattern of home use. Some manufacturers suggest relubrication if the grinder is placed in heavy commercial service.

Because broken wheels are a distinct hazard in bench grinder operation, treat the wheels with more than passing care. One manufacturer flatly declares

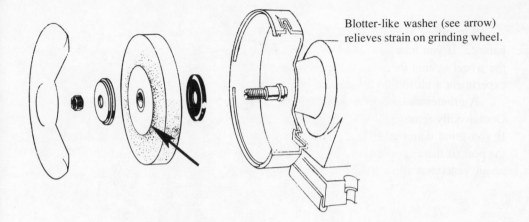

Blotter-like washer (see arrow) relieves strain on grinding wheel.

that *any* grinding wheel that's been dropped should be discarded. It's a good idea, when installing a new wheel, to check it carefully for flaws. To find concealed cracks, hang the wheel on a piece of string and stroke it with a screwdriver handle. If the wheel has a clear sound it's good; a faulty wheel responds with a dull sound.

When replacing a wheel check its rpm rating to see that it's the same as or higher than the nameplate rating of the grinder. A large motor might overstress a wheel that's rated lower. You'll also notice that most abrasive wheels must be installed with blotter-like washers to even the strain of the mounting. Another way to avoid a wheel fracture is to clean the wheel surfaces where they touch the mounting hardware. As you may suspect, abrasive wheels are brittle, so don't use great force in fastening the nut; apply only enough wrench pressure to hold the wheel firmly in place. The motor shaft, or arbor, incidentally, has right- and left-hand threads so that each wheel creates a force which tends to tighten the nut as the motor turns.

Typical hand-held grinder.

Sometimes a spinning wheel develops excessive vibration because of imbalance. If you hear or feel it, stop the motor, loosen the mounting nut, rotate the wheel around the arbor about a half turn, then retighten. You may have to experiment a bit to find the correct orientation to stop annoying vibration.

A grinder sheds considerable debris that may clog its internal mechanism. Occasionally remove the wheel guards to clean the wells of any accumulation. If you grind damp material, matter tends to choke the exhaust port, so check the port (if there is one) for blockage. Underneath the motor housing there may be air vents that also need to be inspected and kept clear.

THE BASIC HAND-HELD GRINDER

This tool is variously called a "hobby," "hand," or "rotary" grinder. Whatever the name, it fits in the hand and is generally wielded like a dentist's drill. Its light weight and small size let you manipulate it in deft, precise strokes on small objects. For this reason it's an excellent tool for the amateur sculptor, wood carver, and jewelry maker and for a dozen other home handicraft pursuits. The instrument can be fitted with dozens of miniature drills, burrs, rasps, abrasive cutters, points, saws, brushes, and polishing wheels. You can match them to almost any medium: wood, metal, ceramic, plaster, leather, glass, stone.

A hand-held grinder attains speeds that often exceed 25,000 rpm. To hold various cutters and points, a *collet* chuck accepts shanks of a specific diameter, such as $1/16$, $1/8$, $3/32$, or $1/4$ inch. Some collet chucks grip more than one shank size, but usually you must change the chuck when changing shank size.

In selecting a small grinder, consider a light-duty model if you want to use the tool mainly for hobby craft work. A housing that's light, easy to grasp—as you would hold a pencil—and well balanced aids the delicate strokes needed for intricate patterns or shapes. Heavier-duty models, which can take large, $1/4$-inch shanks, also serve for hobby work but may not be as comfortable for tiny objects or close quarters. If you are interested in working soft plastic, seashells, or fragile model parts, consider a *variable-speed* grinder for its slow-speed mode of operation. High speeds are best for routing, shaping edges, grinding, engraving, and cutting.

A hand-held grinder should be used with a light touch; otherwise at maximum speed you may remove too much material or stall the motor. Overheating is a signal to reduce the pressure or remove the tip from the work and allow the motor to cool. For most operations you'll feed the work against the rotation of the motor.

Grinder is easily manipulated for exacting work.

A hand-held tool is sufficient for a wide range of tasks—grinding or smoothing metal, shaping soft materials, reaming small holes, or removing rust and dirt from irregularly shaped objects. Several optional accessories afford much greater precision if that's what you need. There is also available a stand to hold the grinder in almost any position, leaving your hands free to control the work exactly.

Another type of stand converts the grinder into a miniature drill press for boring holes with accuracy. A *router* attachment, equipped with a calibrated depth control and edge guide, enables you to create lettering and decorative designs in wood.

Maintaining a hand-held grinder requires little more than replacing carbon brushes, often accessible without disassembling the case. A few drops of light machine oil in the lubricating holes, as prescribed by the manufacturer, helps to keep this intriguing tool running at maximum capacity.

Light-duty grinder is held like a pencil for fine detail.

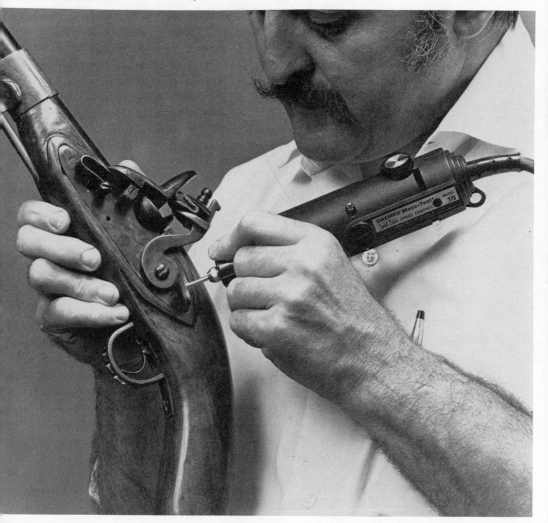

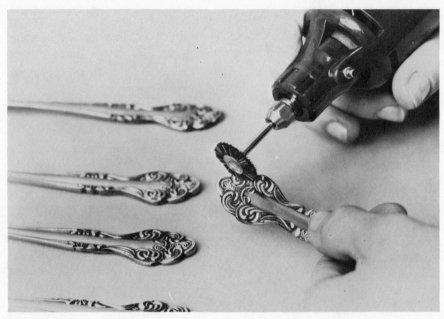

Cleaning silverware with a bristle wheel.

Removing carbon from cylinder head of a small motor with a wire wheel.

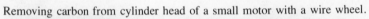

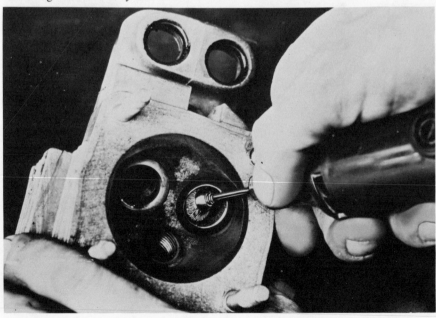

Sanding with a drum sander.

Sanding with a disc sander.

Slotting wood with a steel saw wheel.

Shaping metal with an emery wheel.

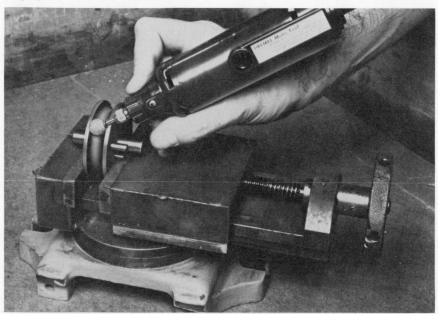

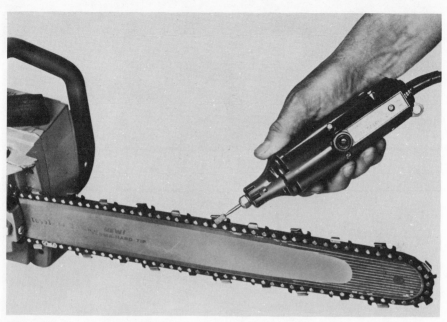

Emery wheel can sharpen chain saw teeth.

Removing flash from a cast metal locomotive with a tungsten-carbide cutter.

Carving cookie molds in wooden blocks.

Cleaning exhaust port of a model engine.

Router attachment enables grinder to carve letters.

8

ROUTER

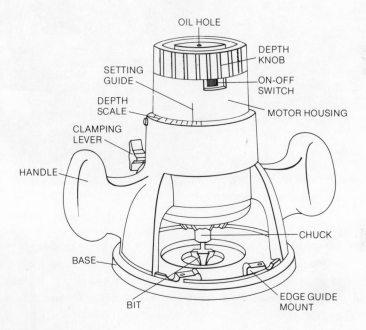

OIL HOLE

DEPTH KNOB

SETTING GUIDE

ON-OFF SWITCH

DEPTH SCALE

MOTOR HOUSING

CLAMPING LEVER

HANDLE

CHUCK

BASE

EDGE GUIDE MOUNT

BIT

Once you've acquired the basic power tools for sawing and smoothing wood, your curiosity will almost certainly be aroused by the router. Until recently this tool was used almost exclusively in the cabinet maker's shop, where it turned out flowing curves, complex contours, and exquisite edges in wood work. To an untrained eye such feats seem wrought by a gifted Old World carver, but this wood-working magic can actually be done in seconds by a router! With models now available anyone of modest talent and matching assets can do the same.

The list of jobs a router can do is almost endless. Take, for instance, a simple panel you've cut to size for a cabinet door. No matter how carefully it's

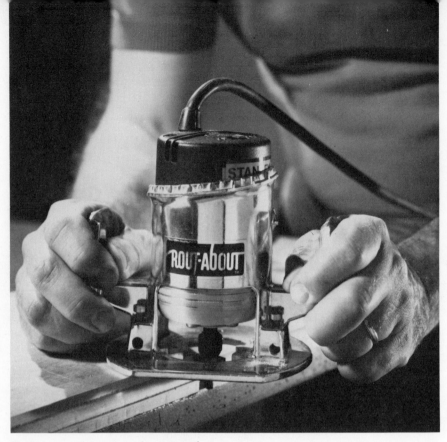
Router cuts a decorative edge on panel.

been sawn and sanded, the piece cannot escape the home-made, sharp-cornered look. But apply a router and you can make dozens of different decorative cuts: rounded, fluted, beaded, reeded. Fancy edge work, however, is only the beginning. A router prepares wood for almost any sophisticated joint, including tongue-and-groove, rabbet, dado, mortise-and-tenon, dovetail, and lap.

Move the tool across the surface and it cuts grooves straight or circular, or irregular shapes guided by your imagination or a template. Such cuts can make the letters of a sign stand out in relief, or form openings for inlaying veneers on a panel. Not only is the router an indispensable aid in shelf construction and furniture and cabinet making, it enables the amateur to plane and shape wood— tasks usually done with more expensive, heavy machinery.

THE BASIC ROUTER

A router, which is among the most versatile of all power tools, is one of the simplest in design. The housing encloses an electric motor that develops

Threads on motor housing (at lower center) enable adjustment of motor height with respect to base.

Large handles at sides of router assure a firm grip.

about $\frac{1}{3}$ to $1\frac{1}{2}$ hp. Supported vertically, the motor shaft points downward and terminates in a collet chuck to grip the bits and cutters that work the material. For convenient bit installation the housing may have a flat top, which can be inverted and placed on a table surface; this frees your hands for manipulating wrenches to tighten the bits in the collet.

With a bit installed, the router is placed on the work and its upper assembly—motor and bit—raised or lowered with respect to the supporting base for desired cutting depth. This can be done using the calibrated depth scale, for an accuracy usually within $\frac{1}{64}$ or $\frac{1}{32}$ inch. A wing nut or other clamping device locks the setting.

Two large handles on the router let you move it over the work free-hand or, more commonly, along a guide. As the router advances on the wood it simultaneously cuts and finishes. Extremely high blade speed enables the bit or cutter to leave a finish that's so smooth it rarely needs sanding.

CHOOSING A ROUTER

There are few special features among various router models. Their differences are mainly in construction, power, and method of adjustment. The majority of models are concentrated in the $\frac{3}{4}$- to 1-hp range, a specification that affects cutting speed. With low-power models you must feed at a slower rate for deep cuts, to avoid loading the motor and thereby slowing it, or run the router over the same area in several passes that bite more deeply each time.

All routers spin at high rates, from about 22,000 to 30,000 rpm; the greater the speed, the smoother will be the cut. While examining the motor, also determine the type of bearings that support the shaft. In low-cost models the bearings are sleeve-type; better routers have ball bearings or a combination of sleeve and ball. If you plan to do extensive routing, ball bearings are recommended—and are certainly the choice for the professional. The occasional user should find sleeve bearings satisfactory for light-duty work.

Are the handles comfortable to grip, and is the depth scale easy to read? Look to see how bits are changed—it should be an easy task. Check that the brushes are readily removable for inspection.

TYPES OF BITS

Some two dozen different router bits should satisfy almost any home wood worker. What is more, by controlling the depth in the wood you can obtain several decorative contours from a single bit. Among the types you'll find are

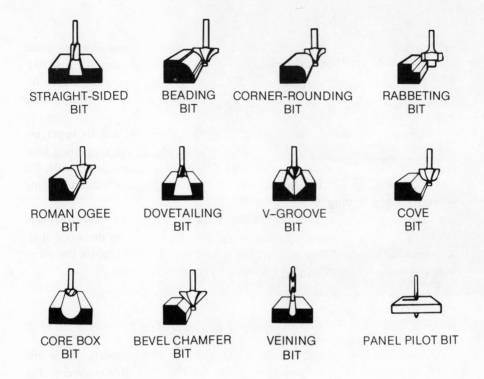

STRAIGHT-SIDED BIT   BEADING BIT   CORNER-ROUNDING BIT   RABBETING BIT

ROMAN OGEE BIT   DOVETAILING BIT   V-GROOVE BIT   COVE BIT

CORE BOX BIT   BEVEL CHAMFER BIT   VEINING BIT   PANEL PILOT BIT

grooving bits, which are lowered to a controlled depth for cutting a variety of shapes. With a *V-groove* bit you can route the familiar ''V'' seen in wall paneling. You can form a semicircular channel with a *core box* bit, and make narrow and shallow grooves with a *veining* bit; that last one is also good for free-hand work. There are *straight-sided* bits to cut square grooves (useful for inlay work), and *dovetailing* bits to make a groove bottom wider than the top; the *rabbeting* bit also falls into the straight-sided group. To speed the job of hanging a door, there's a $^1/_2$-inch-wide grooving bit.

The second major category comprises the *edge* bits. Widely used for trimming edges with a flourish, these bits are usually guided along their path by a *pilot,* a small projection below the cutter portion that slides against the edge of the work. Falling within the edge bit grouping are specialized cutters for trimming veneer and plastic laminate (such as Formica) used for counter tops.

High-strength steel is the bit material most home craftsmen use. With the aid of a bit sharpener you can keep the steel cutting edges in good condition. Harder *carbide-tipped* bits cost about three times more, but they hold an edge

Pilot, at bottom of router, guides an edge bit.

far longer than steel and may be worth the extra money to a serious hobbyist or professional who turns out considerable work.

ACCESSORIES

Some routers come with an adjustable *edge guide* to accurately lead the tool through straight or curved planing, grooving, slotting, and dadoing. It's an important accessory to acquire if your router has none. *Templates,* for guiding the router through an exact pattern, are another useful aid—especially if they are factory-made precision forms. A *dovetail* template, for example, provides the right spacing and depth for dovetail joints in drawer and box construction. If you intend to hang doors, the bothersome part of the job—chiseling out sections to receive the hinges—is neatly done with a *butt hinge* template. *Template guides* are steel bushings that attach to the router to prevent the spinning bit from damaging a home-made template.

You can make your own templates out of plywood by drawing a pattern and then cutting it out. This creates an edge for the router to follow as it cuts the design into the work. For sign making, a router cuts perfect letters about 2¹/₂ inches high using a *lettering template set* sold for the purpose.

Edging operations on curved or irregular pieces of wood may be difficult to guide with ordinary routing methods, but are simple to perform with a *router table*. It's a miniature steel platform with 12-inch legs. The router is bolted beneath the table with the router bit protruding up through a hole in the table sur-

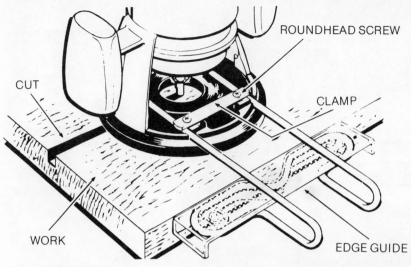

ROUNDHEAD SCREW

CUT

CLAMP

WORK

EDGE GUIDE

Edge guide attachment.

face. Now you can operate the router as a shaper or jointer by placing the wood on the table and pressing it into the spinning bit.

HOW TO USE A ROUTER

A router isn't a dangerous tool, but don't risk skinning your fingers—be sure to disconnect the power cord before changing bits. To install a bit, loosen the collet locknut and insert the shank of the bit all the way into the chuck, then back out about $1/8$ inch. (One manufacturer advises that a $1/8$-inch space prevents the collet from breaking.) Although some collets can be tightened with a single wrench, you may need a pair of wrenches—which are sometimes supplied. One wrench holds the collet chuck while the other tightens the locknut.

Next adjust the depth scale. The details differ from one router to the next, but the general approach is to loosen a clamping arrangement that holds the motor. This allows the bit to be lowered until it just touches the surface of the work. When this happens, the depth scale is calibrated for zero depth. The desired cutting depth is then selected by turning a depth ring or knob against the scale.

When the switch is thrown, there will be a sudden twisting force from the motor, so grasp the handles firmly and don't let the tool get away from you. With a new bit, to avoid any errors on a project you've put much time into, make your first cuts on pieces of scrap lumber. When the trials look good move on to the real work.

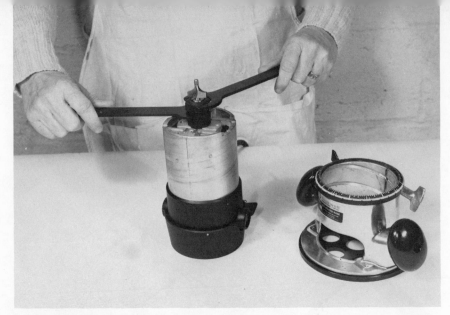

Installing a bit with wrenches.

Pointer shows setting guide for calibrating depth scale.

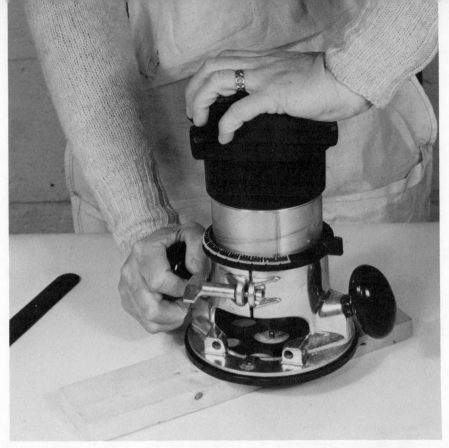

Motor housing is twisted to adjust bit height.

Clamp tightens motor on base
after depth adjustment is made.

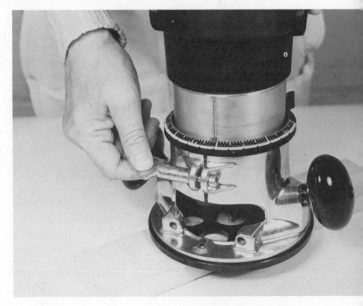

Make a trial cut on scrap. Here bit has cut a rabbet on the edge.

For most decorative edging projects the router nearly guides itself, especially if the bit is furnished with a pilot to bear against the work edge. So long as the router has a firm base to slide on and you don't allow it to drift, the cut takes care of itself. Splintering the wood when you arrive at a corner is avoided by cutting across the grain first, then making those cuts that run with the grain.

Another way to ensure a good finish is to guide the router in a direction that causes the bit to draw itself along the cut—the direction that creates the least chatter. Typically this is the left-to-right direction as you face the work. The cutter then spins clockwise (as viewed from above), turning into the work. Any operation is aided by clamping the work to the bench, if that's practical.

When a router must cut in from the edge of the material, you'll need a mechanical guide. In many instances an edge guide accessory handles the job. Its rods are installed in holes in the router base, adjusted to the desired dimension, then locked with wingnuts. If the edge guide isn't long enough to control the router's path on the work as you want it, clamp on your own straightedge and follow it.

Feed pressure affects a router's cutting speed and, indirectly, the quality of work. When the router is pressed too firmly, rotational speed takes a severe drop and friction increases; this could result in burning the work or the bit. Feeding too slowly, on the other hand, allows the bit to revolve too long in a single area, which can also cause a burn or can result in an uneven or inaccu-

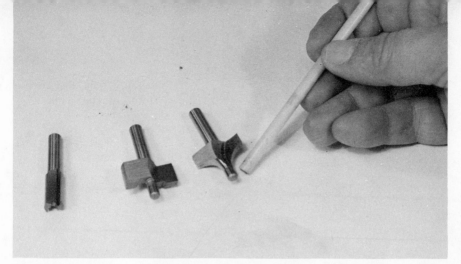

Pointer indicates pilot on bit used for cutting a cove shape. Straight-sided bit is at left, rabbeting bit at center.

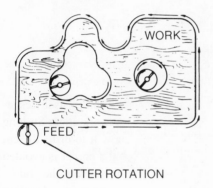

Recommended direction of cut.

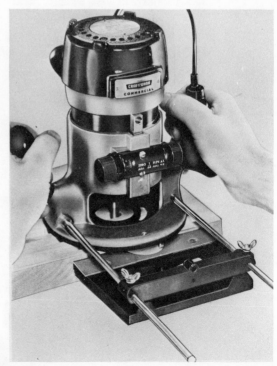

Edge guide accessory in use.

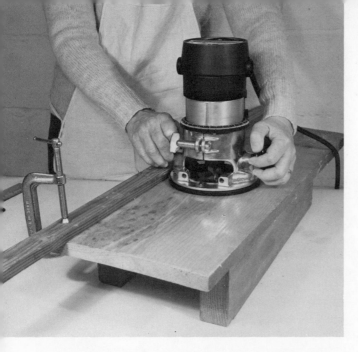

Straightedge can be clamped to the work as a guide.

rate cut. Attempt to develop a light but constant touch, using scrap material, before tackling a serious project. Working hardwood or scoring deep cuts may overload a router, but this problem is overcome by making several passes at increasing depth to lighten the strain on the motor.

Free-hand routing, guided by your artistic ability, can remove background stock to make creative designs stand out in relief. Working in reverse, you can

Free-hand routing follows a pattern drawn on work.

recess the design in the wood. One way to start is to draw the pattern in pencil on the work and remove the waste stock with a veining bit. Be aware that the bit tries to follow the grain; oppose this tendency by firmly gripping the handles. Don't cut too deeply—say, more than $^3/_8$ inch—into the material or the pattern may be difficult to follow. You can also do free-hand lettering on lumber for making signs, but the special template set sold for this gives the job a professional look.

MAINTAINING THE ROUTER

The amount of cooling air reaching the router motor affects its life, so keep air passages free of sawdust—blow them out often when the tool is in service. After about 50 to 100 hours of operation, check the brushes for wear, unless the manufacturer warns that the job should be done at a service center. Bearings are often lubricated for the life of the router and need little attention. A wise investment is a *silicon carbide hone*. The silicon carbide, an exceedingly hard material, sharpens router bits to keep them cutting at peak efficiency.

9

RADIAL ARM SAW

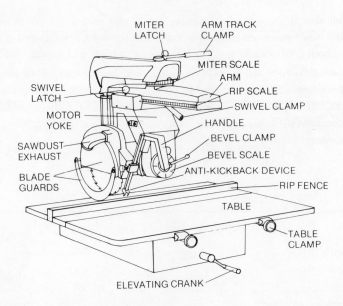

MITER LATCH

ARM TRACK CLAMP

MITER SCALE

ARM

SWIVEL LATCH

RIP SCALE

MOTOR YOKE

SWIVEL CLAMP

HANDLE

SAWDUST EXHAUST

BEVEL CLAMP

BEVEL SCALE

BLADE GUARDS

ANTI-KICKBACK DEVICE

RIP FENCE

TABLE

TABLE CLAMP

ELEVATING CRANK

Complete a few adjustments; place the work on the table; and gently operate the handle. These simple steps are all it takes to run a radial arm saw, a tool of astonishing precision. For years a standard resource of carpenters, builders, and professional wood workers, the radial arm saw has made the transition to the home. Its price is relatively high and it takes up more room in the workshop than other tools, but this saw exerts powerful lures that are difficult to resist. Accuracy is so easy to attain that an amateur's work shows dramatic improvement. Scores of accessories and attachments for special tasks enhance the tool's versatility.

The secret of the saw's capability is in its geometry. With motor and blade mounted in a position over the work, slung from an arm, the whole assembly can pivot and sweep through an almost infinite number of positions. Once the adjustments are locked, the blade tracks through the stock with hairline accuracy. It's especially useful on large or awkward pieces that defy precise cuts with a hand-held saber or circular saw because the chassis supports both the blade and the work. If you want to turn out a number of identical pieces, just clamp a stop on the table; the tool repeats the dimension for each new piece.

The radial arm saw makes each basic cut—rip, cross, bevel, and miter—plus several combinations. It's equally adept at cutting rough lumber and plywood panels, and is especially suitable for furniture making and cabinet work. Add attachments and the tool doubles as a router, drill, jointer, sander, planer, or polisher.

A radial arm saw has its limitations. Its strength lies in its great stability and adaptable blade positioning, but it's not portable. You'll still need independent, carry-about tools, such as a portable saw, sander, and router. Also, the radial arm saw needs plenty of working room. The base doesn't demand much floor space—about a square yard—but you'll occasionally feed long pieces from right or left, so you'll need about 8 feet of access on either side. Sometimes you can gain it by placing the tool next to a door and feeding long items through the opening.

THE BASIC RADIAL ARM SAW

The tool's distinguishing feature is its overhead arm on a rigid vertical column. Suspended from the arm is a yoke bearing an electric motor. The yoke rides in a carriage, or track, along the underside of the arm to carry the motor back and forth as you push or pull a handle. In most models the saw blade bolts directly to the motor shaft, requiring neither gears nor pulleys.

Below the arm is a table surface divided into two or more boards. To act as a guide or stop for the work, a rip fence is inserted between boards and tightened with a table clamp or lock.

Owing to the number of articulated joints in the tool, the blade can be swung and fixed in any plane. Often each strategic adjustment has a calibrated scale to help set the blade at a desired angle. The swing of the arm about the vertical column, for example, is indicated by a miter scale. As you angle the blade with respect to the work placed against the rip fence, you can choose the desired number of degrees. Once you've made the choice, a lock fixes the blade position.

Typical saw has overhead arm
and rigid supporting column.

Hands hold blade guard, which is adjustable. Top hand holds sawdust exhaust.
Anti-kickback device is attached at right end of guard.

For simple cross cutting, the blade is held at right angles to the long dimension of the work and moved backward or forward. To make a rip cut, the blade is unclamped and rotated for alignment with the work's long dimension. On some models a rip scale appears along the side of the arm to indicate where the kerf (cut) falls. The depth of a cut is adjusted by an elevating crank, usually calibrated against a scale. For bevel cutting, motor and blade are tilted in the yoke; again, a scale may aid in setting up the saw for the desired angle. Most calibrated scales also provide detents—pins which snap into a preset position—to help you quickly locate the most commonly used angles of 0, 45, and 90 degrees.

An anti-kickback device is a standard attachment on a radial arm saw. Metal fingers suspended from the blade guard trail the work surface during a ripping operation. The work moves through the blade and under the fingers with little opposition, but a kickback, wherein the work reverses direction, causes the fingers to dig into the wood and arrest its motion.

SPECIAL FEATURES

A blade brake is a premium aid on a radial arm saw. It's offered in two versions: a *manual* brake lets you reduce the time to halt a coasting blade after power is turned off, while more advanced models have an *automatic* brake that self-activates when you switch off the power.

A standard radial arm saw is wired for 120-volt house current. Heavy-duty models, however, draw considerable amperage, which may cause a voltage drop that affects the tool's performance. To offset the drop some manufacturers provide an option of 240-volt operation. You must, however, supply a special line to the tool to make use of this feature.

An exhaust or spout for sawdust is attached to the blade housing on most models. In many saws there is also a *vacuum* connection. Attach a shop vacuum cleaner to this point, and both clean-up time and the amount of dust floating in the air are reduced.

CHOOSING A RADIAL ARM SAW

Radial arm saws are rated according to horsepower from about 1 to more than 3 hp. Because high-power saws are aimed at the professional, a light or intermediate model is sufficient for the home hobbyist unless there is need for much continuous cutting. Blade diameters, which increase with horsepower, run about 8, 9, and 10 inches. A 10-inch blade may be important to some operators for cutting four-by-four lumber, but it's not essential for the amateur. The heaviest wood you're apt to saw is of a standard 2-inch thickness (which is actually closer to $1^1/_2$ inches), and any model can do it in two passes. The work is turned over for the second pass.

Look for a saw's depth of cut as stated in the manufacturer's literature. At 90 degrees (where the blade is perpendicular, or straight up) different models cut from $2^1/_2$ to 3 inches deep. When the blade is tilted for a bevel cut at 45 degrees, maximum depth may be reduced to 2 or $2^1/_2$ inches, depending on blade diameter. Note that in any case you can still cut the popular 2-inch framing lumber.

If you opt for a heavy-duty model, the special 120/240-volt power option could become attractive. A large motor operating continuously over long periods may lose efficiency when fed from a lengthy 120-volt line. Moderate-size home saws, however, run efficiently on a standard 15-ampere branch circuit. If you feed work to the blade too forcefully, the motor may draw a surge of power through the line and exceed 15 amps. Brief overloads like this are tolerated if you install a time delay fuse or breaker at the service entrance box.

The motor in a radial arm saw is of either the *universal* or the *induction* type. The latter has some slight advantages: it runs more quietly and without motor brushes and armature commutator—items in a universal motor that may wear and need attention or replacement. Either motor type generates dangerous forces that should be controllable by an on-off switch you can easily reach in case of emergency. The guard over the upper half of the blade affords some protection, and some models add a lower guard that floats over the work and helps conceal the blade in that area. To prevent the saw from harming other people when you're away, most models are provided with a locking arrangement—key switch or padlock—for security.

As the price of a radial arm saw increases, certain features improve in quality. The table is thicker, and greater mechanical rigidity improves cutting accuracy. On a large table the maximum ripping width may rise from 20 to 26 inches and the maximum span of a cross cut may go from 18 to 22 inches. One deluxe feature on higher-priced saws is a number of extra spindles for running accessories at various speeds. Most notable is a 20,000-rpm spindle that develops the high rates required by routing and shaping attachments.

ACCESSORIES

A combination blade is standard equipment supplied by radial arm saw makers—an acceptable compromise for routine cross cutting and ripping. For finer or faster results, blades with specialized teeth are better. A *hard-tooth* combination blade is one improvement for fast, accurate cutting of hardwood and plastic. By adding lubricant to the work, the blade also handles lightweight aluminum and other soft nonferrous metals. When you plan to do repetitive, production-type work, an expensive *carbide-tipped* blade can return its value in long service life.

Consider a *rip* blade if you'll do considerable rip cutting, or simply if you want to make the job easier. *Plywood* or *planer* blades work through plywood and other stock so smoothly that sanding may not be required. They're helpful on furniture and other projects that demand a fine finish.

Another class of attachments accomplishes more sophisticated cutting jobs. To add a professional touch to your shelf making, acquire a *dado set* (see page 156). This blade assembly mounts on the saw arbor. It cuts precise slots in wood to support shelf ends. A dado set has two outer cutting blades, which sandwich inner chippers. In a single pass across the work, the dado set cuts a channel from about $1/8$ to 1 inch wide. Forming a tenon—a tongue-like projection on the edge of a piece—is also possible using this set, with the chipper blades removed and spacer washers installed in their place.

Saw on open-frame stand.

A *molding cutter head,* a spinning attachment that takes an assortment of cutting knives, creates thousands of decorative molding shapes. With a *rotary planer* you can quickly clean up old lumber or size boards.

Wood finishing is made easier by a variety of attachments. A *disk sander* removes material quickly and smoothes surfaces and end grains; it also creates bevels. A *drum sander* is helpful for straight and curved edges and delicate sanding jobs. If the saw motor has a high-speed auxiliary shaft, consider a *router bit* for cutting grooves and other shapes.

Several other accessories make the tool more convenient to operate. You can buy an open-frame stand or a steel cabinet with drawers and compartments for stowing loose blades and other items. Some bases accommodate *casters* so that the saw can be easily rolled to another location to provide more space when cutting large pieces. Finally, don't overlook a *sawdust collector*—a plastic shroud that catches waste and directs it to a bag or box below the chute.

HOW TO USE A RADIAL ARM SAW

Try a cross cut for the first operation. After clamping the rip fence securely on the table, be sure the blade is locked in line with the arm. A carpenter's square can be used to check whether the blade is at right angles to the fence and perpendicular to the table surface. These relationships must be accurate or every piece of stock you attempt to cut will be affected.

Next consider blade height. Turn the elevating crank to lower the blade so that the edge is about $1/8$ inch below the underside of the work. At this depth the blade cuts slightly into the table surface and through the rip fence on the first pass, creating valuable reference lines on the table and fence to show the actual track made by the saw.

To start a cross cut, don't turn on power but grasp the handle and move the blade beyond the rip fence, near the vertical column. Place the board on the table and press it evenly against the fence, preferably with the left hand. (For safety's sake never put your fingers close to the blade.) When you line up the pencil line on the board with the slot in the rip fence, remember that your saw blade has width; you want to place the kerf on the waste side of the work.

When you're satisfied with the work alignment on the table, turn on the motor and pull the blade toward you through the rip fence and the work. Go slowly and feel for the blade's best cutting pressure—too much force produces a rough cutting edge. After the blade clears the work completely, push forward

Cross cut.

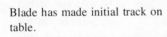

Blade has made initial track on table.

Rip cut.

and return the blade to the starting position. Turn off the motor. You'll be amazed at the simplicity of the operation and the quality of your handiwork.

With certain materials the blade should be *pushed* rather than pulled. Pushing may work better for extremely hard or thick (3-inch or 4-inch) lumber and for aluminum. When cutting thick material you may not have enough blade surface to accomplish the cut in a single sweep. This problem is solved by making one pass, then inverting the work and passing through a second time. You must carefully align the work before the second pass to be certain the two cuts match and merge into a single line.

The second important operation is the rip cut—cutting with the long dimension. Unlike cross cutting, in ripping you move the work, not the saw. The blade is placed parallel to the rip fence and locked at the desired width of the finished piece. During the set-up you should adjust the anti-kickback device. The chances of kickback, a danger in a ripping operation, can be reduced by lowering the curved fingers of the device until they just contact the surface of the material. After the fingers are locked at the correct height, they won't impede the blade's progress—unless a kickback suddenly changes the direction of feed.

Never feed work toward the edge of the blade that bears the anti-kickback device. The work must travel toward the *rising* edge of the blade (there's often an arrow imprinted on the blade to show direction of rotation).

To start a rip cut, place the board flat on the table and align its edge with the rip fence. Feed the material gradually into the blade, using the fence as a

Miter cut.

Bevel cross cut.

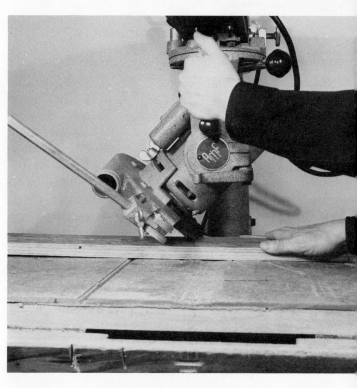

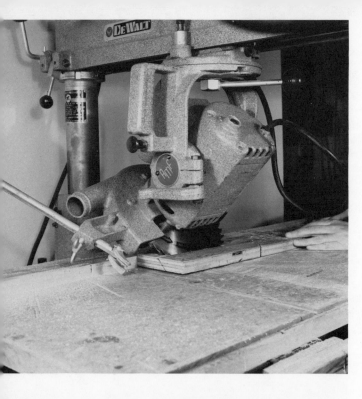

Bevel rip cut.

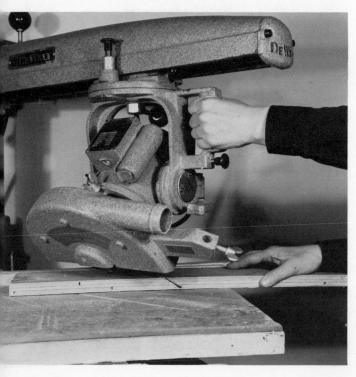

Compound miter cut.

guide. As the work progresses, your hand moves closer to the blade, so be wary of the cutting path. Always use a *push stick* when the work is narrow or your hand tends to move dangerously close to the blade. Some saws have a movable blade guard you can lower to afford further protection against accidental contact with the blade. Once the cut is completed turn off the power, but wait until the blade halts before you remove the work.

A miter cut is basically a cross cut, with the overhead arm swung to a desired cutting angle. After the required number of degrees is selected on the miter scale near the top of the arm, pull the blade through the work as described above for cross cutting. Cutting a bevel is done by following the general procedure for ripping, except that the bevel clamp handle is loosened, the blade adjusted to the desired degree of slant, and the assembly resecured with the locking clamp.

Making use of these basic cuts, the blade's maneuverability, and the assortment of special accessories, there are few cutting operations that can stymie the radial arm saw.

MAINTAINING THE RADIAL ARM SAW

The saw blade should be checked occasionally for proper alignment. Dust and dirt create abrasive action in the moving parts, which causes inaccuracies to creep into the tool's performance. Occasionally, determine if the blade is

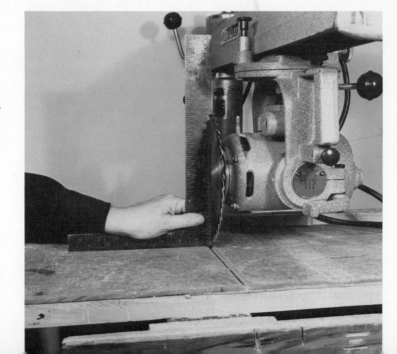

Checking accuracy of blade mounting.

still square with the table surface by placing one edge of a steel carpenter's square against the edge of the blade, and the other edge of the square on the table. Any discrepancy can usually be corrected by loosening the motor bracket and squaring the blade manually. When this is done the miter scale should read zero. If the scale is incorrect, you can on some models loosen the indicator and reset it to zero.

The blade must also move evenly across the table as it travels toward the rip fence. Again, a steel square placed on the table and pressed against the rip fence produces a straightedge that serves as a reference line. The blade should track that edge from start to finish. Adjustments are usually provided on the tool so you can make any tracking compensation.

Maintenance is usually a minor matter with a radial arm saw—especially if your model has an induction motor, with no brushes to wear out. Follow the manufacturer's instructions; he may warn that the track (in the arm) is never to be oiled, but that the elevating arm mechanism, miter latch, and bevel clamp require machine oil.

Keep the tool clean. It generates much sawdust and works better if the arbor flanges (large washers that sandwich the blade), air openings, and various moving surfaces are periodically wiped clean of grease and dirt.

10
LATHE

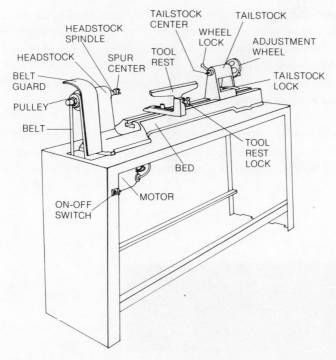

HEADSTOCK SPINDLE
TAILSTOCK CENTER
TAILSTOCK
WHEEL LOCK
HEADSTOCK
TOOL REST
ADJUSTMENT WHEEL
SPUR CENTER
BELT GUARD
TAILSTOCK LOCK
PULLEY
BELT
TOOL REST LOCK
BED
ON-OFF SWITCH
MOTOR

Mention the word "lathe" and you think of a master craftsman hewing wood into exotic forms. The image is fading, however, as more amateurs discover the satisfaction of creating esthetic objects at home on a simple machine. The power lathe can turn bowls, table and chair legs, columns, chess pieces, knobs, lamp bases, and other such objects. It works in wood, plastic, and soft metals like aluminum, brass, and copper. Attach some accessories and the lathe will sand, drill, buff, and polish. It takes skill to become an artist on a lathe, but even a beginner can turn out satisfying work almost immediately.

THE BASIC LATHE

As you face the machine, you'll see four prominent parts. A massive section at the left is the headstock. It supplies mechanical support and driving force to one side of the work. The headstock, which remains rigidly in position, houses a motor-and-pulley arrangement to rotate the headstock spindle.

At the right side of the lathe is the tailstock, also with a spindle. As the supporting member for the other side of the work, it slides back and forth to accommodate the length of the piece to be turned. The tailstock rides on the horizontal bed, the third major component. The bed is flat or tubular, depending on the particular design.

For the lathe to engage and turn the work, the spindles on either side are fitted with centers. At the headstock side a spur center with sharp projections bites into the piece to apply positive driving force. At the other end the tailstock center presses a point into the piece to serve as an axle.

The last major part is the tool rest. Clamped in various positions with respect to the work, it supports the chisel tools that remove material as the work spins.

Spindle turning—the method just described—isn't the only way to manipulate work on a lathe. If a piece has a disk shape, such as a bowl, instead of being fixed between centers it is suspended for *faceplate turning*. The work is

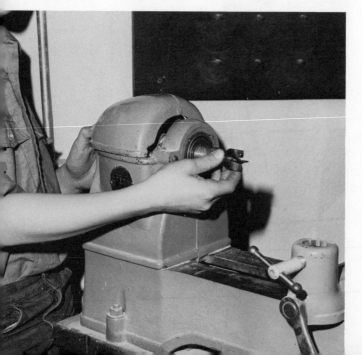

Headstock, with hand showing spur center.

Adjusting tailstock center.

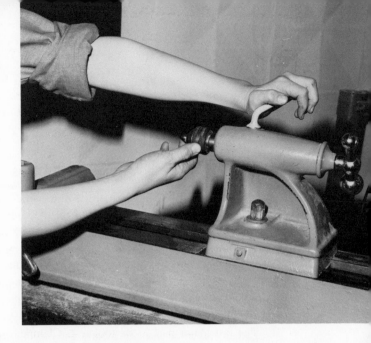

Adjusting tool rest.

fastened (by screws or glue) to a plate driven by the headstock. Some lathes have a *bed gap,* or depression, near the headstock so the lathe can turn large-diameter work that would otherwise be blocked by the bed.

CHOOSING A LATHE

If a lathe is called "10-inch," the dimension refers to the largest diameter it can "swing" over the lathe bed. In other words, the spindles on a 10-inch lathe lie about 5 inches above the bed. The second important specification is the distance between spindles because it governs the maximum length of any piece you install. This dimension is about 36 inches (or a little more) to hold one of the most commonly turned objects—the table leg. Typical lathes for home craftsmen are rated "12 by 36" and "10 by 37," either size offering enough capacity to handle almost any job.

Lathes for home use are mostly for turning wood. Metal-working lathes are massive, expensive, and almost strictly for industrial use. There is, however, a miniaturized version of a metal-working lathe that has proved extremely popular among model makers and hobbyists wanting to fabricate small metal, wood, or plastic parts. The model shown in the illustration can be used for free-hand or precision turning of pieces up to $6^{1}/_{2}$ inches long. With a provision for swinging the headstock to a vertical position, it can also be used for precision drilling, milling, and surface grinding. These miniature models have proved especially attractive to gunsmiths, watch makers, and research labs engaged in prototype design because they turn out intricately shaped parts to tolerances as close as $^{5}/_{1000}$ inch. Their small overall size (about 18 inches long) makes them convenient to operate on a tabletop.

Miniature lathe for metal and wood working.

Pulley and belt for controlling speed.

Lathes are generally powered by a motor-and-pulley that provides four basic spindle speeds. Stock of large diameter requires a low speed, while smaller items are turned at higher rates. A spindle speed chart usually supplied by the manufacturer suggests the ideal rpm rate for metal turning, wood boring, buffing, sanding, and free-hand turning. With the advent of solid-state electronic controls, some lathes are available with continuously variable speeds from 800 to 2800 rpm, eliminating the need to change belts.

The motor is generally installed in a wood lathe after purchase because there's a choice of power rating and type of bearings for the same basic tool. A heavy-duty motor might be rated at $^1/_2$ hp and come equipped with ball bearings for rugged service. For the home handyman a less expensive $^1/_3$-hp motor with sleeve bearings would probably be sufficient. A typical motor turns at a basic 1725 rpm, but stepped pulleys on the spindle and in the headstock commonly allow for the following outputs: 990 rpm, 1475 rpm, 2220 rpm, and 3250 rpm.

Examine the bed of a lathe because its stability affects your work. To achieve rigidity and low vibration, professional lathes have heavy cast iron beds. A well-constructed bed of steel tubing, however, may be all an amateur needs. Move the tailstock over the rails to check for smooth, gliding motion. You should be able to make each lathe adjustment with precision and ease and then lock it securely. Look at the headstock. It should be sufficiently sturdy to

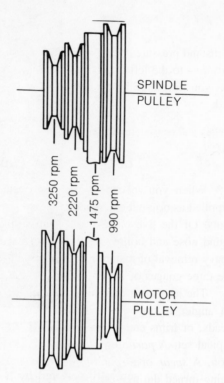

Pulley spindle speeds.

SPINDLE
PULLEY

3250 rpm
2220 rpm
1475 rpm
990 rpm

MOTOR
PULLEY

Lathe with tubular bed.

withstand pressures developed in turning heavy materials. Can you mount work *outside*—to the left of the headstock? Known as *outboard turning,* this feature lets you turn large bowls and other wide items that can't swing over the lathe bed.

CUTTING TOOLS AND ACCESSORIES

When you've chosen the basic lathe, consider attachments that aren't supplied as original equipment. The most immediate need is for a set of turning tools. Of the five basic chisel shapes, the most useful is the *gouge*. With a round nose and hollow shaft, it works well for roughing operations requiring heavy removal of material and for cutting cove shapes. In the typical chisel set are three gouges of increasing width—$\frac{1}{4}$, $\frac{1}{2}$, and $\frac{3}{4}$ inch.

The next most important shape is the *skew,* a flat chisel with its end cut at an angle. It smoothes cylinders, cuts V-grooves, squares shoulders, forms beads, or trims ends. Two skews, of $\frac{1}{2}$- and 1-inch width, are supplied in a typical set. A *parting tool* makes incisions and sizes cuts to a desired dimension. A *spear* or a *round-nose* chisel is chosen to match the contour of work being turned during scraping (a technique described below). These chisels are manufactured in high-speed steel for wood working; more expensive carbide-

An assortment of wood-turning tools.

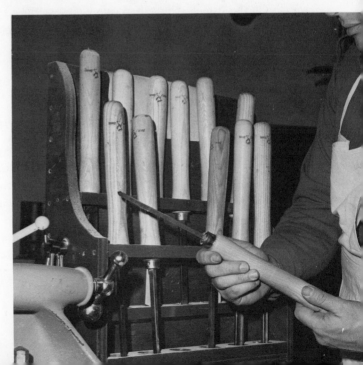

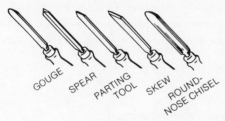

Basic lathe chisels.

GOUGE   SPEAR   PARTING TOOL   SKEW   ROUND-NOSE CHISEL

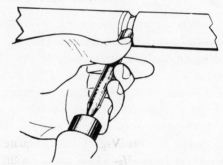

A gouge is used for a cove cut.

tipped equivalents are available for aluminum, copper, brass, mild steel, and plastic as well as wood.

After you've turned some basic projects, various accessories may prove attractive. You can purchase a *faceplate* to attach to the headstock for making bowls and other objects that can't be suspended on the usual centers. To do buffing, sanding, grinding, and polishing, consider a *work arbor,* which holds the attachments for these jobs. A shaft at one end of the work arbor is screwed to the headstock spindle for driving power. The other end of the arbor can grip a sanding wheel, drum, or other attachment. Several different chuck types are also sold as accessories for horizontal drilling.

HOW TO USE A LATHE

Spindle turning, with the work mounted between head- and tailstock, is the most common lathe operation. It's done using either of two basic techniques—scraping or cutting—depending on the choice of tool, how the tool is held, and your skill. Scraping, however, is the easier approach for the beginner. To prepare wood for turning, mark each end for its true center. Draw diagonals at the ends if the piece is square; use a combination square to find the center of a circular piece. At the headstock side insert a spur center in one end of

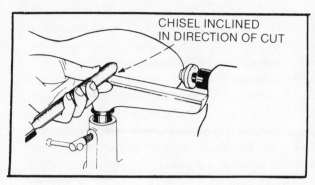

CHISEL INCLINED
IN DIRECTION OF CUT

Spindle turning.

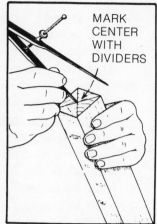

MARK
CENTER
WITH
DIVIDERS

Marking center.

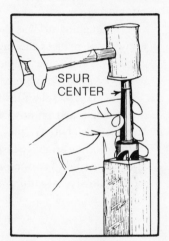

SPUR
CENTER

Installing spur center.

Lubricate contact point between
work and tailstock center.

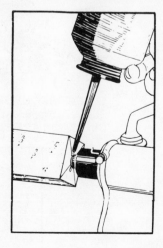

the wood, pressing it in or driving it with a mallet. If the wood is hard, drill pilot holes or make shallow saw cuts to seat the center. After the spurs are embedded in the wood, that end is installed on the headstock spindle.

At the other end move the tailstock toward the wood until the center just touches and holds the work. Continue to adjust the tailstock until the work starts to bind as you rotate it by hand. Back off the adjustment wheel by about one half turn so that the piece freely revolves about the tailstock center. Because the tailstock center usually doesn't rotate, apply oil or graphite to reduce friction at the contact point between wood and center. This isn't necessary if you use a ball-bearing center, which turns with the work.

Grasp the mounted work with your hand and give it a few turns to see if it strikes any lathe parts. Only when you're sure everything is snug and locked in place should you apply power. If the piece vibrates excessively, speed is probably too high.

"Roughing off" is the first basic step in the turning operation. Done with a gouge, it reduces the raw stock to a cylinder. Next a parting tool might be applied to mark the cylinder along its length with the outlines of decorative curves or other design elements.

As shown in the illustrations, the amount of stock removal depends on the gouge angle and on how the tool is moved over the work. *Scraping* removes less material but has the advantage of easier control in a beginner's hands. *Cutting,* or shearing, is faster and creates a smoother finish, but it takes experience to master. For scraping, the gouge is held approximately level and advanced slowly. A cutting operation is done with higher tool angles against the work.

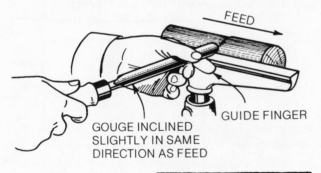

FEED

Roughing off.

GUIDE FINGER

GOUGE INCLINED
SLIGHTLY IN SAME
DIRECTION AS FEED

Cutting and scraping.

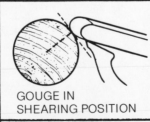

GOUGE IN
SHEARING POSITION

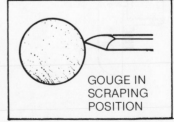

GOUGE IN
SCRAPING
POSITION

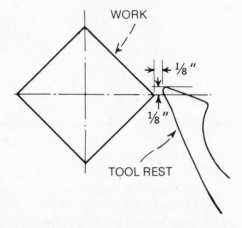

Recommended tool rest position.

WORK

1/8 "

1/8 "

TOOL REST

Although there is no exact position specified for the tool rest, a good start-ing location is slightly above the centerline of the work and 1/8 inch from its edge. If the rest is too low the chisel may chatter. Forcible kickback of the chisel is aggravated by several conditions—the rest may be too low and the chisel angle too high, or both the rest and the tool may be riding too high on the work.

To make an item like a bowl, the faceplate is mounted to the headstock and the work fastened with small wood screws. If the screws interfere with the turning operation, cure the problem by mounting a backing block on the face-plate, then gluing the work to the block with a sheet of paper in between. The paper lets you separate the work from the block later without damage. Another helpful procedure is to bore a large hole into the stock with a wood bit to remove as much waste material as you can before turning. Then you can rough

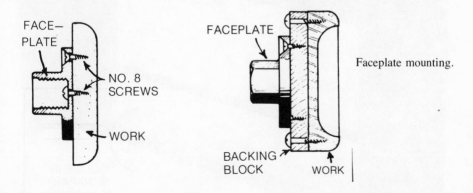

FACE—
PLATE

NO. 8
SCREWS

WORK

FACEPLATE

BACKING
BLOCK

WORK

Faceplate mounting.

Faceplate turning.

out the hollow area with a round-nose chisel or gouge to within about $^1/_8$ inch of the final depth. The sides of the hollow are finished by scraping with a spear or skew chisel. The bottom is smoothed with a flat-nose chisel.

This is just a sample of the intricate, delicate work you can do with a lathe. With some experience you'll turn oval pieces (by mounting the work off-center), make attractive half- or quarter-round pieces by cutting them from full-circle turnings, or fashion wooden rings and balls with the aid of a template.

Lathe mounted on steel stand.

MAINTAINING THE LATHE

The tool is so simple it needs little attention, especially if it has sealed ball bearings. Occasionally check alignment of the centers. Because the spur center at the headstock must meet the tailstock center, an adjustment to correct an off-center condition is sometimes necessary.

If the lathe tends to tip over, slide across the floor, or "walk" when you apply a cutting tool, correct the instability by securing the lathe to a bench or to the floor. Finally, have an oilstone handy. With a few swipes you'll keep chisel edges in good condition.

11

TABLE SAW

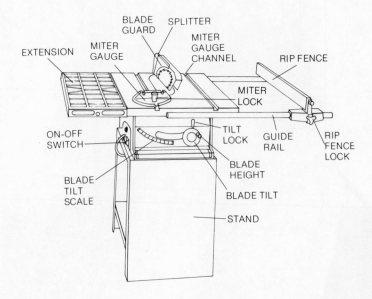

EXTENSION · MITER GAUGE · BLADE GUARD · SPLITTER · MITER GAUGE CHANNEL · RIP FENCE · MITER LOCK · ON-OFF SWITCH · TILT LOCK · GUIDE RAIL · RIP FENCE LOCK · BLADE HEIGHT · BLADE TILT SCALE · BLADE TILT · STAND

With moderate skill a beginner can turn out pieces of extraordinary accuracy using a table saw. Much of the workmanship is already machined into the tool by the manufacturer. A table saw is a mechanical marvel that guides its blade with unerring accuracy through each basic cut—rip, cross, bevel, and miter. Besides reducing stock to desired basic dimensions, the saw performs scores of cutting and shaping operations on pieces of all sizes.

The table saw is not, however, the ideal first purchase for the novice. It is among the most expensive power tools for the home, and it occupies several square feet of floor space. Also, many of its wood-working functions are similar to those of a radial arm saw, and the decision as to which of the two to acquire is often difficult. The principal advantage of a table saw is that it places almost no restriction on the width of material it cuts. You can rip a large panel in half, for example—a job that's not often possible within the confines of a radial arm saw. On the other hand, a radial arm saw is easier to manipulate through operations like cross cutting. You'll have to make the final choice of the tool that best suits the type of work you'll do.

Table saw accommodates large pieces of stock.

THE BASIC TABLE SAW

The central feature of the saw is a broad table, sometimes furnished with wing-like extensions on either side. Only a small part of the blade is visible because it is mounted below the table and protrudes through a slot. The blade is turned by a concealed motor through belts or by direct drive from the motor shaft. As you face the saw, the top of the blade rotates toward you and presses the work against the table surface. When the work is fed to the blade a protective guard is gently prodded out of the way to expose the teeth. (Note that the blade guard in other illustrations here is removed for the sake of clarity.) Just behind the blade there may be a *splitter,* which holds the edges of the kerf slightly apart to eliminate binding as the blade passes through.

The blade is highly maneuverable in two planes. A *tilt* control cants the blade with respect to the table for bevel cutting. A *height* control adjusts the extent that the blade protrudes through the table channel to match the material's thickness. Both the tilt and height controls are preadjusted by handwheel or lever to the desired setting, often against a calibrated scale.

Plastic guard, near center, covers saw blade to protect operator.

Wheels adjust blade height and tilt.

Two devices accurately guide the material through the blade. One is the *rip fence,* which runs from front to back and lies parallel to the saw blade. To rip a piece of stock, the long edge of the work is steadied against the fence and the end pushed through the blade. The width of the cut is preset by unlocking the rip fence and sliding it toward or away from the blade.

The other guiding member is a *miter gauge* for making cross cuts through the piece's short dimension. Sliding in a channel from front to back, the miter gauge holds the piece at an angle with reference to the saw blade.

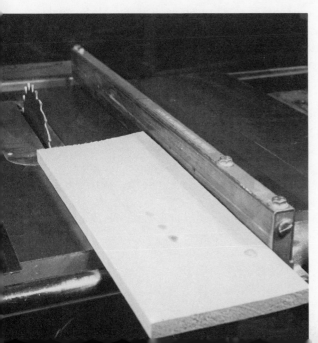

Rip fence (at right) guides stock.

CHOOSING A TABLE SAW

Because the tool has made a transition from the industrial to the consumer market, carefully note how prices are quoted. Large power tools are offered to commercial customers without such basic elements as the motor to allow latitude in setting up and using the tool for a desired function. When looking at table saws, therefore, determine if the price tag includes the motor. Another variable is the outboard table extensions; they too may not be included as original equipment. A stand supporting the table saw is another optional item.

Consider the power source. Most tools for a home craftsman plug into a 15-amp wall outlet, but a table saw may have a special requirement, such as a separate 20-amp circuit. This could call for an extra line brought in by an electrician. Sometimes the saw manufacturer supplies no power switch to control the tool—it is installed as a separate item.

A major consideration in selecting a table saw is blade diameter. Generally offered in four sizes from $7^1/2$ to 12 inches in diameter, the choice of blade determines maximum cutting depth, as follows: blade diameter $7^1/2$ inches, cutting depth $1^5/8$ inches; blade 9 inches, depth $2^1/8$ inches; blade 10 inches, depth $3^3/8$ inches; blade 12 inches, depth $3^9/16$ inches.

Even the smallest-diameter blade, limited to a $1^5/8$-inch depth, cuts common two-by-four lumber because the "two" is actually $1^1/2$ or $1^5/8$ inches. The next most important dimension in framing lumber is 4 inches. If you expose a stud in an older house, chances are that "four" inches is $3^5/8$ inches. More recently the lumber industry narrowed this trim size to $3^1/2$ inches. (Nothing makes an old-time carpenter more irascible than a home improvement in which old and new two-by-fours are mixed.) If you plan to cut much four-by-four lumber (frequently used as supporting posts), a large-diameter blade might prove attractive. But even using the smallest table saw you can do the job if you make one pass, invert the piece, carefully align the blade with the cut, then make a second pass. For decorative work or furniture and in cabinet making, stock is rarely more than $1^1/2$ inches thick and so can be cut by a $7^1/2$-inch table saw.

Motor horsepower ranges between 1 and 3 hp. A hefty 12-inch model with a $3^1/2$-hp motor powered by 220 volts is available; it takes a mighty load but is hardly an item for the home handyman. A 9- or 10-inch table saw is more practical. Within this blade category there's a range of horsepower (which hovers around 1 hp) that affects how fast the blade passes through the work. Higher horsepower works faster but costs more.

Two types of motor drive table saws: *universal* and *induction*. Somewhat less expensive, the universal motor is often noisier and requires a belt connection to the saw blade. The induction motor found in higher-priced models is quieter in service and connects directly to the blade with no intervening belt. There's less maintenance, too, because carbon brushes and a commutator are absent.

A *blade guard* was once an optional item, but the trend is to furnish it as standard equipment. Study the blade guard—does it respond easily to work moving into the blade, and does it afford good protection for your fingers? See if the guard obscures your view of where blade and work join. Some guards let you peek at the guideline through an open slot, often a good arrangement, while others rely on clear plastic to reveal the cutting area. Examine how the manufacturer protects you from moving parts such as belts or exposed teeth underneath the table.

Another protective device on a table saw is an *anti-kickback* mechanism. It suspends metal fingers onto the work as the material moves through the blade; any tendency for the work to shoot toward you is arrested. Spring loading of the fingers, found on some models, may improve their seizing action.

The switch that powers a table saw has been improved by designers to prevent an unwitting turn-on by you or a curious child. Protruding "ears" around the switch deflect a hand that accidentally brushes the switch. To prevent tampering by others, these ears are often pierced by holes to take a padlock.

Sturdy support is essential for safe operation. That's why this tool is often called a "bench saw"—it occupies a stationary mount on the floor. The bench is not an integral part of the machine, and the quoted saw price does not usually include the stand. It is possible to install the saw on your own bench, or you can obtain a separate base or stand to support the tool. Be sure the base isn't wobbly—especially if you intend to install casters on the legs to wheel the saw over the floor.

Much of the pleasure of using a table saw is in the ease with which you can set up the tool before starting. To see if a particular model measures up in this regard, inspect its blade operating controls. Are the tilt and height adjustments convenient? They should strike a good compromise between ease of setting and fineness of measurement. A desirable feature is an error-correcting adjustment to bring into agreement the calibration mark and the actual blade position. The tilt control may have built-in stops to enable quick setting of the blade to the commonly used angles of zero and 45 degrees.

The two important guides for rip and miter operations should be convenient to adjust. When the rip fence is clamped in position it must always lie

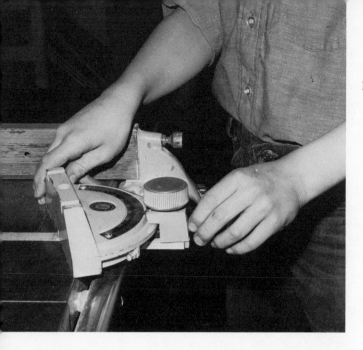

Miter gauge.

Table saw and base stand.

Work is angled by miter gauge (at right).

parallel to the saw blade; unless you can set it accurately your work won't be precise. There are several other adjustments on a table saw that are internal and require only occasional service. When they do need attention, it helps to have an owner's manual that plainly tells how to perform the job.

BLADES AND ACCESSORIES

If a new saw comes with a blade, it will be a combination type. This general-purpose blade handles both cross and rip cutting and may remain mounted on the saw for most work. Only when you do considerable cutting of one type is it practical to purchase a rip- or cross-cut blade. A hollow-ground *planer* blade makes very smooth cuts for mitering or trimming. If you want extremely long life in a blade, consider a carbide-tipped version, though it's priced much higher than high-speed steel types. Metal cutting is done with an abrasive blade, but check the manufacturer's literature on this point. Some abrasive blades can break apart in metal cutting.

After blades, the most interesting accessories for a table saw are attachments for making dadoes and moldings. A dado is cut by a blade set consisting of two outside blades that sandwich several *chippers*. When mounted on the arbor in place of the conventional blade, the dado set cuts grooves from about $1/8$ to $13/16$ inch. It's a useful cut in making shelves, joints, rabbets, and tenons.

Dado set consists of two outer blades and several chippers between them.

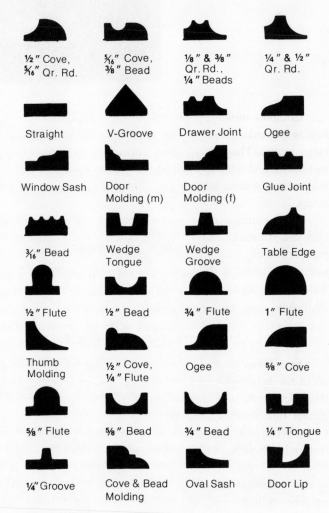

½″ Cove, 5⁄16″ Qr. Rd.	5⁄16″ Cove, 3⁄8″ Bead	⅛″ & 3⁄8″ Qr. Rd., ¼″ Beads	¼″ & ½″ Qr. Rd.
Straight	V-Groove	Drawer Joint	Ogee
Window Sash	Door Molding (m)	Door Molding (f)	Glue Joint
3⁄16″ Bead	Wedge Tongue	Wedge Groove	Table Edge
½″ Flute	½″ Bead	¾″ Flute	1″ Flute
Thumb Molding	½″ Cove, ¼″ Flute	Ogee	5⁄8″ Cove
5⁄8″ Flute	5⁄8″ Bead	¾″ Bead	¼″ Tongue
¼″ Groove	Cove & Bead Molding	Oval Sash	Door Lip

Molding Styles

Table inserts change width of blade slot for accessory cutters.

Complex moldings are formed with a *molding cutter head*. The head section is a circular piece that fits on the saw arbor and is fitted with a variety of cutter knives. The knives can cut almost any molding style for table edges, cabinet doors, and windows. When you purchase dado or molding attachments you must obtain special table inserts that modify the slot for use with these accessories.

Table extensions are another valuable accessory. The basic table for a 9-inch saw is usually 22 by 17 inches, which is a small area when handling large pieces of stock. This area can be expanded by bolting extension wings on either side of the table. A stable extension adds about 9 to 12 inches to overall table width, while an adjustable extension, which slides on rods, can reach as far as 20 inches.

HOW TO USE A TABLE SAW

In order to get the smoothest results, adjust the blade so that its teeth rise about the height of a tooth above the thickness of the work. An exception to this rule occurs with hollow-ground blades, which cut best when they rise to greater than tooth height above the work. Check the manufacturer's instructions. When you position work on the table, place the "good" side up. The teeth initially strike the "good" side, which should suffer the least splintering, from above, cut through, then cause some shredding as they exit from the work's underside. After the work is on the table, align and press it against the rip fence or miter gauge, depending on the cut.

Blade is most often adjusted to about one tooth height above work.

Stay alert while operating a table saw. Don't risk injury by what fighter pilots call "target fascination"—when the pilot becomes so mesmerized by the sight of a plane he's tailing that he follows it into the ground. Keep your eyes skimming over the whole job. *Never* position your hands so an inadvertent slip could carry them to the blade—and don't attempt to cut in free-hand fashion. Always support the piece against a guide. After the work is cut in two, you'll have a free and a supported piece (the latter against the guide). It's hazardous to grasp the free piece before the blade stops.

Let's try rip cutting. If the work is narrow (say 4 inches or less) there's a risk of running your fingers too close to the blade. This is easily overcome by a simple safety device you can make in a few moments. It's a *push stick*—a piece of wood about 12 inches long with a notch in one corner and a handle at the other end. Instead of gripping narrow work with your fingers, hook the notch over the top edge of the work and push. Press the stick with downward and forward pressure (as you would push a lawn mower) to move the work toward the blade. Another way to avoid the blade is to habitually raise your hands high as you withdraw them over the table at the end of the cut.

The rip scale is adequate to set up the fence for an ordinary rip cut, but if you want high accuracy verify the dimension with a rule placed on the table. A trick to achieve precision is to make a trial cut or two on scrap lumber. When the rip fence is in good alignment it reduces binding and kickback; but in case they do occur remember not to stand directly in front of the blade.

Pushstick for ripping narrow pieces.

Hand position while ripping stock.

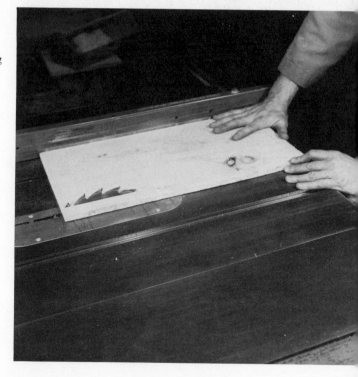

Cross cut with miter gauge at 0
degrees.

Cross cut with miter gauge at 45
degrees.

Most workers place the rip fence on the right side of the blade and guide the stock toward the blade with one or two hands, keeping fingers well clear of danger. Another technique is to press the work against the fence with the left hand while the right applies forward pressure. Lift either hand if it moves uncomfortably close to the blade.

Prepare for a cross cut by setting up the miter gauge. The device rides in either table channel, but it's most often placed on the left side (as you face the tool). Loosen the locking knob and set the gauge at zero for a regular cross cut, at 45 degrees for a miter cut, or at some other desired angle. Built-in stops help you quickly locate the most commonly required settings. Again, if the job demands close accuracy verify the miter angle with a square after tightening the locking knob. When you tilt the blade for a bevel cut, decide if the miter gauge should be in the right or left groove—whichever interferes least with your hand and the blade guard.

In a cross cut, feed the work with the same caution you'd use in a ripping operation. With the edge of the wood held against the miter gauge, move the stock into the blade until it is cut in two, then pull the work back to the starting point. Just before pulling back, move the work slightly away from the blade. Don't use the rip fence for a measuring check when you're cross-cutting a piece to a given size, because the piece could jam between fence and blade.

MAINTAINING THE TABLE SAW

If the saw motor stops during a cutting operation, you may have triggered a built-in overload relay. This happens if you apply too much feed pressure or if the blade is dull. To restore power, switch off the motor and let it cool for 3 to 5 minutes. Push the reset button, turn on the switch, and resume working. Another reason to keep the blade sharp is to reduce any tendency to kick back.

A table saw's accuracy hinges on its adjustments. From time to time use a square to confirm proper alignment of the tool's various elements. The blade must be perpendicular to the table and parallel to the miter gauge slot. When in the zero position the gauge must be at right angles to the blade and must ride parallel to it. The rip fence should be parallel to both the miter gauge slot and the blade.

In time, excessive wear in the mechanism may raise the blade. You can spot this condition when you note that cutting height doesn't stay constant. Caused by backlash, the problem is usually curable by following the manufacturer's instructions on how to eliminate mechanical play in the height assembly. Follow his instructions, too, on changing brushes, if your machine has them. A general rule is to check brushes after the first 50 hours of saw operation, then every 10 hours thereafter. Brushes that are worn down as much as about $^1/_4$ inch should be replaced.

12
SCROLL (JIG) SAW

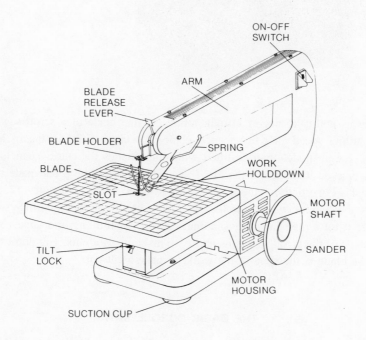

Manufacturers variously call this tool a "scroll" or a "jig" saw. Sometimes "scroll" designates a large saw of the type, while "jig" refers to a small saw for model making. The tool has a slim blade that cuts with short up-and-down strokes. Because the blade is narrow it can follow intricate, irregular curves in wood, metal, seashell, ivory, and many other materials, which makes a scroll saw popular for crafts like jewelry making, scroll work, and pattern cutting. Youngsters not yet able to handle other power tools can operate such a saw with little danger because blade travel is so limited.

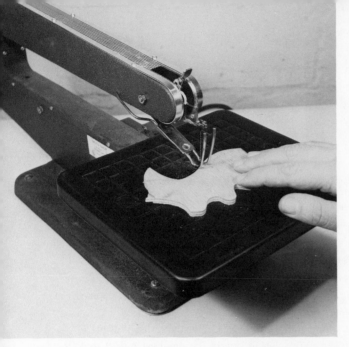

Jig saw excels at cutting curves.

In its ability to negotiate tight turns, the fine blade of a scroll saw sacrifices cutting speed. It's not a good choice for large-scale ripping of lengthy pieces. Large models can be fitted with thick blades for cutting panels, shelf stock, or even lumber, but the tool's specialty is the curving cut made in light material. (For contour cutting in heavy lumber, refer to chapter 13, which covers the band saw.) A scroll saw is also useful in rough-cutting stock to prepare it for a finer finish by sanding, carving, or turning on a lathe. Another advantage of the scroll saw is its ability to make interior cuts; you don't have to start the blade at the edge of the work to make a cut-out.

THE BASIC SCROLL SAW

An overhead arm supports the top end of a scroll saw blade. About 5 inches long, the blade drops through an opening in the table and is attached at the bottom to the drive system. Motive force is applied in different ways, but the blade is always driven up and down with reciprocating motion. Spring tension on the upper end keeps the blade straight and taut between a pair of chucks. In some models the blade may be temporarily gripped and supported solely at the bottom to perform saber-saw cutting jobs. A blade guide under the table keeps the blade from yielding under pressure of the work.

Besides supporting the work, the table can tilt the stock for bevel cutting. A spring-loaded hold-down presses the work against the table to restrain it against vibration, which would reduce the cutting action. Because most operations are done in free-hand fashion, a scroll saw may have no provision for a built-in rip fence to guide the work.

CHOOSING A SCROLL SAW

A key specification is throat size—the space between the blade and the rear support arm. Ranging from about 10 to 26 inches, the throat limits maximum stock size. In large models, however, the arm is removable for saber sawing, so there's no restriction on stock size. Another feature that overcomes limitations set by throat size is a rotatable blade; it lets you feed long lengths from the side rather than toward the arm. The other important scroll saw capacity is depth of cut—typically between 1 and 2 inches.

Scroll saws fall into three approximate categories. These overlap, but price differences are significant and you may wish to obtain the smallest model that can handle the work you prefer to do. First is the simple tool usually called a jig saw, aimed at the hobbyist interested in making model airplanes and other objects of light material. The overhead arm that holds the blade is little more than a U-shaped piece of spring steel; vibrating motion is furnished by magnetic impulses, which operate the blade at about 7200 strokes per minute. A good starting tool for a youngster, it's a light-duty machine for thin wood, aluminum, and copper.

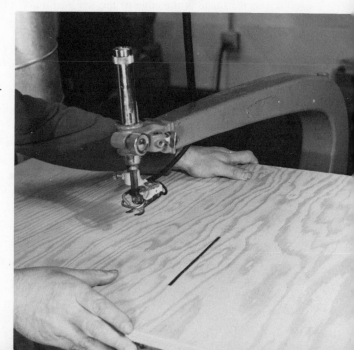

Scroll saw has large throat size. Blade is seen lying on wood, near bottom center.

Hobby type of saw. Note sanding disk at lower right.

Large scroll saw.

Pulley and belt for changing saw speed.

The next step up is an intermediate-size scroll saw, with a 15-inch throat and built-in motor. The motor operates a rocker assembly to impart reciprocating motion and drives an output shaft for external accessories. The variety of possible accessories makes this model extremely versatile—a miniature power shop that saws, sands, grinds, buffs, polishes, and carves. The machine's sawing capacity, or depth of cut, may be up to $1^3/_4$ inches in softwood, $^1/_2$ inch in hardwood, and $^1/_4$ inch in aluminum, 18-gauge copper, and $^1/_{16}$-inch steel. A scroll saw in this class usually takes 3-inch ''pin'' blades that engage in holders at top and bottom.

The third class includes the large scroll saw found in a professional woodworking establishment or the shop of an advanced hobbyist. In this model a 16-inch throat and a cutting depth of at least 2 inches are typical. As for commercial-grade tools, the motor is sold separately in different sizes to suit the customer. A home user, for example, might choose the lightest-duty drive—a $^1/_3$-hp motor with sleeve bearings. A heavier-duty version has ball bearings and $^1/_2$-hp motor. Blade speed in large tools is adjustable through a stepped belt-and-pulley arrangement that yields three or four speeds between 600 and 1700 rpm. In some models a variable-speed control system enables any rpm selection over a continuous range.

BLADES AND ACCESSORIES

Some two dozen different blades are offered for scroll saws. They vary according to width and number of teeth per inch but fall generally into two categories: *jeweler* and *saber*. The former type, used for intricate curves, mounts in the saw's top and bottom chucks. Wood is usually cut with a blade of 15 or 20 tpi, while copper, brass, and aluminum require about 20 tpi. Very fine work on materials like seashell is done with jeweler-type blades of 30 tpi. For heavy cutting, choose the thicker blades in the saber category. Attached only at the bottom (with the saw's upper arm removed), they do a faster cutting job on heavy pieces.

RECOMMENDED BLADE SELECTION FOR SCROLL SAW		
Application	Blade Width (in.)	Teeth per Inch
Steel, iron, lead, copper, aluminum,	.070	32
pewter, asbestos, paper, felt	.070	20
Steel, iron, lead, copper, brass,	.070	15
aluminum, pewter,	.085	15
asbestos, wood	.110	20
Asbestos, brake linings, mica, steel, iron,		
lead, copper, brass, aluminum, pewter	.250	20
Wood veneer, plastic, celluloid, hard rubber,		
Bakelite, ivory, extremely thin metals	.350	20
Plastic, celluloid,	.050	15
hard rubber, Bakelite,	.070	7
ivory, wood	.110	7
Wallboard, pressed wood, wood, lead,		
bone, felt, paper, copper, ivory, aluminum	.110	15
	.110	10
	.187	10
Hardwood, softwood	.250	7
Pearl, pewter, mica,	.054	30
pressed wood, seashell,	.054	20
jewelry, metal, hard leather	.085	12

If you plan to use a variety of blade sizes, consider purchasing replacement guides, if available, to augment the one supplied with the original tool. Guides are made with different-size openings to accommodate a particular blade thickness.

A useful accessory is a sanding attachment on a flexible cable. Fitted with fine or medium abrasive sleeves, the sander gives a final finish on delicate concave, convex, or flat surfaces.

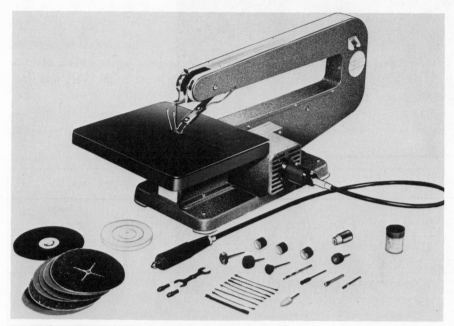

Sanding and grinding attachments with flexible cable.

HOW TO USE A SCROLL SAW

The rule-of-thumb in choosing a blade is to select narrow blades for highly detailed work and wide blades for straight runs or gentle curves on large pieces. The narrower the blade, however, the more difficult it becomes to control and steer precisely through the work. Pick the widest blade that easily follows the desired curve.

Check blade adjustment before starting up. After it's mounted in the chucks, the blade must run in the guide without excessive friction. If a blade is fine, tension should be greater than for heavy types, but don't overdo it—too much tension snaps a thin blade. After the blade is in place, eye it from both front and side to see if it's running vertically. The table should also lie at a right angle to the blade (unless you're cutting an angle).

On some saws you can adjust the tension of the hold-down spring that presses the work against the table. The spring fingers should prevent a chattering sound when the blade is running. There should be just enough pressure to hold the work without digging into it. As you make a test cut to see if adjustments are correct, check whether the machine tends to "walk." For a tabletop model the manufacturer may supply suction cups to absorb noise and vibration, but additional quieting is possible by placing a rubber pad under the tool.

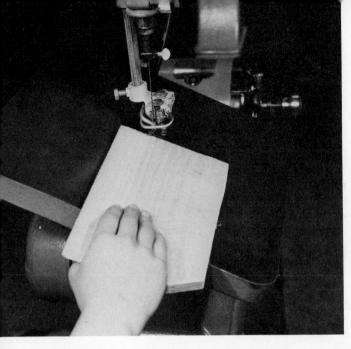

Table is tilted for bevel cutting.

You can feed the work into a scroll saw from different positions and angles, but try this starting technique: place your left hand on the work to guide it along the cutting line; use your right hand to push the work against the blade. Never apply a sudden twisting force, or the blade may warp and break. Another blade-snapper is forcing the work too fast. Let reciprocating action, not forward motion, do the cutting.

If your work emerges with a splintered, ragged edge, there are several possible causes. Thin stock tends to break up along the bottom edge of a cut; place a piece of scrap under the work to prevent this. Another reason may be that the blade is too coarse and is snagging against the work edge. This can be avoided by selecting a blade that can simultaneously place at least three teeth against the edge of the work. Sharp blades are important too. You can solve the problem of a dull blade by changing table height—it brings a fresh set of cutting teeth into play.

Much scroll work is done by following a pattern marked on the piece. You can paste a pattern on the stock and begin cutting, but you'll destroy the pattern. If you wish to preserve it for future use, trace the lines on the stock with carbon paper. If any part of the work needs an internal cut, try *piercing*. Drill a small hole in one corner of the desired cut-out, insert the free saw blade through the hole, then secure it to the blade chucks.

Straight cuts can be done free-hand, but if accuracy is important clamp a straightedge on the table to serve as a guide. If the piece is long and threatens to strike the overhead arm, reinstall the blade so it is parallel with the front edge of the table. This allows you to rip stock of any length, provided the width is not greater than that of the throat area.

Metal cutting requires a special blade and slow speed. If thin sheet metal tends to curl when it is cut, sandwich it between two pieces of thin wood and saw the three pieces as one assembly. When cutting metal lubricate the blade with beeswax to prevent excessive friction. Unfortunately you can't reduce heat with a lubricant while cutting many plastics; even as you cut, the heat tends to weld the plastic together behind the blade. To prevent overheating of plastic work, run the saw at the slowest possible speed and use the coarsest blade.

13

BAND SAW

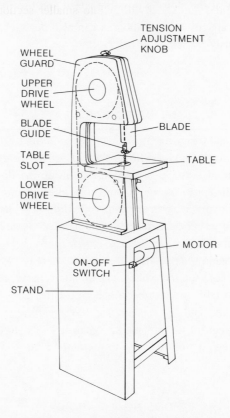

WHEEL GUARD

UPPER DRIVE WHEEL

BLADE GUIDE

TABLE SLOT

LOWER DRIVE WHEEL

TENSION ADJUSTMENT KNOB

BLADE

TABLE

MOTOR

ON-OFF SWITCH

STAND

At first glance the band saw appears to be first cousin to the scroll saw. Both tools have narrow, vertical blades that are adept at cutting curves in wood. But the resemblance doesn't extend much further. A scroll saw thrusts in short, reciprocating strokes; the band saw sweeps in a continuous loop over two large wheels, which enables the blade to slice through stock faster than any other conventional cutting tool.

Speed is only one of the band saw's attractions. Because of the great distance between the drive wheels, the tool has enormous depth capacity. While most saws can cut wood only up to about 2 inches thick, a band saw handles wood 6 inches thick. The machine is especially handy in wood-working shops where straight or curving cuts in extraordinarily heavy lumber are necessary. Another valuable use for a band saw is cutting blanks, or rough shapes, for turning on a lathe. This spares the lathe worker much of the roughing-off labor required to get rid of excess material.

Still another band saw job is *re*sawing. You can pass a heavy board through the blade and quickly divide it into smaller sections. With the tool's yawning vertical capacity, several boards can also be stacked on the table and sawed simultaneously for identical pieces.

THE BASIC BAND SAW

The tool is a stationary machine that weighs 50 to 100 pounds; most of its working parts are supported by a floor stand. The interior of the tall housing is filled with the pair of massive drive wheels. Inside the floor stand below, an electric motor applies power to the lower drive wheel through a pulley and belt. Riding around the two wheels is an endless flexible saw blade about 5 to 8 feet long, depending on wheel diameter and spacing. The blade rides on thin rubber tires mounted on the rims of the wheels.

To keep the blade running true, the upper wheel is adjustable for the right amount of tension between the wheels. The blade is prevented from running off the wheels by adjustable guides above and below the table. A calibrated tilting mechanism locks the table at a slant for bevel cutting; you can choose the desired angle between blade and work. When it's time to change the blade it can slide free through a slot that runs to the table edge.

CHOOSING A BAND SAW

The quoted size of a band saw is based on its wheel diameter. A "10-inch" model has about a 10-inch wheel and a throat capacity of the same size. This allows you to place 20-inch-wide stock on the table and rip it in half. Another important specification is maximum depth of the cut. All but the smallest band saws accept 6-inch-thick stock. Capacities of some typical models are as follows: $9^{1}/_{2}$-inch wheels, $4^{1}/_{2}$-inch cut; 10- to 12-inch wheels, 6-

Ten-inch band saw with steel base.

inch cut; 14-inch wheels, 6¹/₂-inch cut. Heavy-duty band saws range to 18-inch size, but the diameters given above should be satisfactory for the home user.

Blade speed, rated in fpm (feet per minute), is concentrated in a range of 2000 to 3000 fpm. There's not much choice here for the buyer because the speed is usually coupled to saw size—for example: 10 inches, 2400 fpm; 12 inches, 2900 fpm; 14 inches, 3000 fpm. Higher speeds make smoother cuts, but this can depend also on the choice of blade. Another factor related to saw

Calibrated scale below table for adjusting table tilt.

Arrow shows large throat capacity of a typical band saw.

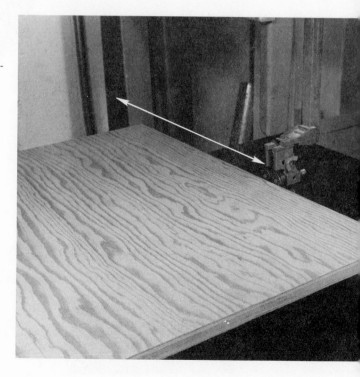

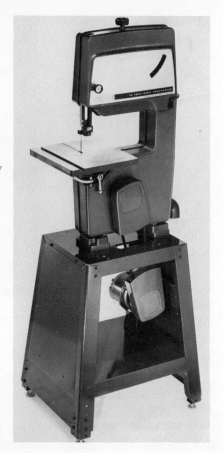

Motor, mounted below in stand, is usually installed as a separate item.

Miter gauge is an accessory. Table must have groove to receive it.

Rip fence, an accessory, is seen attached
to table at right.

size is the range of blade widths a machine can accept. If you choose an average-size band saw, you can install blades of from $^1/_8$-inch to $^1/_2$-inch width. Wider blades are an asset when cutting heavy stock because the thickness of the blade helps to straighten the kerf.

Because a band saw motor is ordered as a separate item, there is some leeway in choice of horsepower. Three typical motor sizes are $^1/_4$-, $^1/_3$-, and $^1/_2$-hp. Check the manufacturer's recommendation; where he allows a choice, the most powerful drive will probably cut the fastest. Motor quality also varies—sleeve bearings are suitable for moderate service, while ball bearings stand up better under the rigors of commercial operation.

Several band saws have tables that can receive optional accessories. If you wish to add a miter gauge, look for a groove in the table to hold it. Also check whether the table is fitted to receive a rip fence. Accommodations for both these accessories are found only on large band saws. On a moderately priced tool you can, however, rig a substitute cutting guide from clamps and strips that is adequate for occasional use.

TYPES OF BLADES

There's a blade for almost any cutting job. Depending on its width and number of teeth per inch, a blade can follow tight-radius curves, or move rapidly through heavy wood. Generally speaking, the faster the blade, the less smooth the cut. Here is a typical blade selection: for fine scroll cutting, $^1/_8$ inch with 15 tpi; for plywood, $^1/_8$ to $^1/_4$ inch with 15 tpi; for ordinary wood, $^1/_4$ to $^1/_2$ inch with 6 or 7 tpi; for nonferrous metal, $^1/_4$ inch with 10 tpi. Within these categories you can also purchase *skip tooth* blades. They have fewer teeth (lower tpi), to keep the kerf free of sawdust and the blade moving faster.

Thick blades are less prone to breakage, but as width increases a blade loses ability to follow curves. The minimum cutting radius for some typical blades is as follows: $^1/_8$ inch wide (6 tpi), $^1/_4$-inch radius; $^3/_{16}$ inch wide (6 tpi), $^1/_2$-inch radius; $^1/_4$ inch wide (6 tpi), $^3/_4$-inch radius; $^3/_8$ inch wide (5 tpi), 1-inch radius. These blade sizes, incidentally, comprise a good selection for the home workshop.

If the manufacturer prohibits metal cutting in the instructions for his band saw, don't attempt it because friction may be excessive. Hard materials require a special speed reducer attached to the saw.

HOW TO USE A BAND SAW

Many operations with a band saw are done free-hand. You'll push the work through the blade following a pattern drawn on or transferred to the stock. Start by guiding the work along the cutting line with your left hand as the right hand applies forward pressure. When a curve changes direction your hands may reverse these roles, but the general idea remains the same. An important precaution: don't move your hands directly along the blade's line of cut, so that in case of an inadvertent slip your hand will not skid into the blade.

A band saw blade is flexible and can't take much forcing against the work—it may bend or even break. Use gentle pressure and a slow feed. When you arrive at a curve remember that the blade could twist out of alignment if the turning radius is too tight. Either relax feed pressure or install a narrower blade that can follow the sharp turn.

Avoid pressing hands directly into blade. Note how table is angled for a bevel cut.

Straight cuts as well are often done free-hand. It helps to use the widest possible blade because width increases cutting stability along the line. For cutting very accurate straight edges with a saw that has no rip fence, improvise your own guide using a straight piece of wood or metal clamped to the table.

You can use a band saw in several ways. Try *stack sawing*—placing several boards on the table, one on the next, and running the blade through them all for a production-type run of identical pieces. *Blanking* is another helpful process; it removes massive sections of waste to prepare for refining of the stock with a slower-cutting tool such as a sander or lathe. Blanking eliminates much tedious cutting. Try *compound* cutting—sawing away sections from two different planes of the stock. (A table leg, for example, may have dissimilar curves or lines on adjacent sides.) To do this, draw the desired patterns on the top and side of the stock. Cut out one pattern, then temporarily rejoin the waste pieces with tape to support the work while cutting out the pattern in the second plane.

During curving cuts the work may strike the tool's rear support and prevent further cutting in that direction. You may have to backtrack to start the cut from a different angle or entry point. To avoid this as much as possible, make the shortest cuts first, anticipating before you begin how the work might strike the support. You can often figure a direction of feed for the quickest pass through the blade with the least backtracking.

MAINTAINING THE BAND SAW

Blade tension needs special attention when blades are changed. Because each blade demands a different setting—that is, a narrower blade needs higher tension—adjustment is necessary. Some band saws have a scale with pointer built into the machine as a reference; in this case follow the manufacturer's specifications. In simpler models use your judgment. Here is an approximate guide rule: proper tension exists when the blade can flex about $1/4$ inch over a span of 6 inches. Avoid too much tension (a common pitfall) because the blade needs sufficient pressure so that it won't slip on the drive wheels. One tip to prolong blade life, if you want to take the trouble, is to relax blade tension when the saw won't be in service for a long period.

Your work won't be accurate and blades won't last their full life if blade tracking is improperly adjusted. Check it by turning the upper wheel by hand and watching the blade; it should remain centered on the wheel. If tracking is not true, adjust screws on the upper wheel to bring the blade into line. Blade

Keep rims of drive wheels clean.

guides, which keep the cut straight, have brackets that are adjustable, so that when inserting a new blade you can bring the guide very close to it.

Sometimes a blade won't cut straight because its teeth are dull or damaged from striking metal (usually a nail embedded in the work). Often a faulty blade can be sharpened or reset at a reasonable price locally, but some manufacturers suggest that buying a new blade is more economical than resharpening an old one. It's a matter of individual choice.

A band saw needs occasional lubrication. In some models the upper wheel has needle bearings that take light machine oil. Blade supports, however, often have ball bearings and remain lubricated for the life of the machine. Table *trunnions,* or pivots, located underneath the table, need a light oiling to keep moving parts operating freely.

Gum and pitch tend to accumulate on the tool's rubber tires and blades. Occasionally remove these contaminants with detergent to keep the saw in top condition.

14

CHAIN SAW

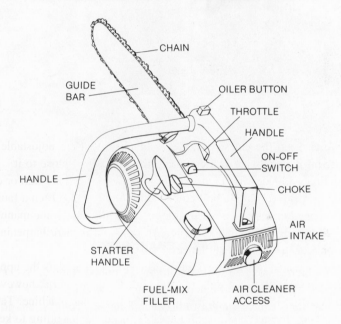

CHAIN

GUIDE
BAR

OILER BUTTON

THROTTLE

HANDLE

ON-OFF
SWITCH

HANDLE

CHOKE

AIR
INTAKE

STARTER
HANDLE

FUEL-MIX
FILLER

AIR CLEANER
ACCESS

As the nineteen-sixties drew to a close, tool makers witnessed a remarkable shift in the chain saw market. Before that time a chain saw was a tool hefted by lumberjacks to fell timber somewhere in the North Woods; but now ordinary people began to buy the saw in such great numbers that by the seventies more than half the industry's output went to nonprofessionals. The chain saw's popularity is easy to explain. Even with occasional use, a homeowner can quickly recover the cost of the tool by doing his own pruning and trimming, cutting firewood, clearing dead trees, or building rustic projects. A whole new hobby, ''chain saw carpentry,'' has sprung up that exploits the tool's ability to sink through heavy logs with little effort.

"Bucking," or cutting a log into lengths, is done with speed and ease.

THE BASIC CHAIN SAW

Popular chain saws are a far cry from the 24-pound Bunyan-size models in the lumberjack class. For the homeowner a typical saw is constructed of light metal and plastic to reduce weight to between 8 and 13 pounds, and it is powered by a nimble 2-cycle engine that runs on unleaded gasoline from the neighborhood service station. Lubricating oil is usually mixed with the gasoline in a ratio of about 16 parts gasoline to 1 part oil.

Engine power is delivered to a centrifugal clutch that holds the chain motionless until you open the throttle and accelerate to over 3000 rpm. At these speeds, weighted shoes inside the clutch are moved apart by centrifugal force; they expand within a drum and deliver motive power to a toothed sprocket. This arrangement not only allows you to stop and start the saw without stopping the engine but adds an important safety factor: if the saw is suddenly seized or obstructed, the clutch stalls, reducing chances of injury.

The teeth of the sprocket operate the chain, or cutting end, of the saw. Forming an endless loop, the chain consists of links flexibly riveted together

Typical compact model.

and fitted with drive tangs and cutters. The tangs pick up motive power from the sprocket while the cutters penetrate the wood. Cutters have a precise shape enabling them to simultaneously slice the wood, clean the cut, and carry away sawdust.

The *pitch* of the chain is critical, especially at replacement time, because it determines whether the chain will fit on the sprocket. Pitch is determined by measuring the total distance of three successive rivets (anywhere on the chain) and dividing by 2. Another important specification is the chain's *gauge,* or thickness of a drive tang. If it's too wide the chain won't mount properly or will lack good cutting action and control. With too narrow a gauge, sawdust may foul the action.

Kerf is the width of the cut made as the cutters sweep across the wood. The manufacturer matches the kerf to the engine power and chain length of the particular model. As kerf increases, higher engine power is required to deliver an efficient cut in a given hardness of wood. A wide kerf is often selected by professional operators for cutting softwoods like pine and cedar; a narrow kerf is the best choice for cutting hardwoods like Douglas fir and walnut.

The chain encircles a *cutting bar,* or *guide,* for support. The guide, a thin hardened-steel plate, has rails around its edges to create a groove for the chain. Internal passages carry oil for cooling and lubricating between the guide and chain. Most friction occurs at the nose (far end) of the guide, so this area in expensive, high-powered models is often fitted with special alloys or a roller bearing. All chain saws have a button to allow the operator to inject oil into the cutting bar and chain at frequent intervals.

An array of knobs and levers controls the chain saw. Starting and stopping are effected by an ignition switch; a choke produces the rich fuel mixture necessary for cold starting; and a starter rope flips the engine to create spark and draw fuel into the combustion chamber. The throttle turns the engine up to about 10,000 rpm—dropping to about 6000 rpm as the saw cuts under load.

SPECIAL FEATURES

Chain saws are manufactured in a broad range of models, from a stripped-down "price leader" to the more elaborate "top-of-the-line" model with a full complement of special features. Price boundaries often correspond to variations in power and size, but a number of other equipment differences can appear anywhere in a particular line. Some of the more significant features offered by chain saw producers are described below.

Automatic Oiling. The cutting bar needs oiling every few minutes—or even seconds—as the chain races in its groove at high speed. Studies show that some operators forget to press the oiler button, so designers have contrived an oiling system that automatically injects lubricant. It's a useful feature, but it doesn't completely eliminate the need for manual oiling. Even with automatic oiling you must press the button when cutting extremely dry wood or under an extra-heavy load.

All-Position Carburetor. With this feature you can hold the saw upside down without stopping fuel flow to the engine. It's especially valuable for pruning, where you'll often swing the saw into an odd position that would normally interrupt power.

Throttle Latch. Some saws apparently need three hands to start. A throttle latch lends a mechanical hand, holding the throttle partly open while you grasp the saw and pull the starter rope. The latch releases as the engine starts and you manually accelerate the throttle.

Compression Release. Another starting aid, this valve in the combustion chamber opens to release part of the pressure built up by the piston. Effort needed to pull the starter rope is consequently reduced by approximately one half.

Muffler. Some saws exhaust spent gases through a simple stack, while more elaborate models have a muffler to keep chips, sawdust, and dirt out of the exhaust port. A muffler also quiets to some degree the raucous sound of a

2-stroke engine turning at maximum speed. Some mufflers include spark arrestors to reduce the threat of fire in dry brush.

Built-In Sharpener. Keen cutters are virtually assured with this accessory. Sharpening is done when you press a button while the chain is rotating. Even with this feature, however, a saw needs occasional sharpening using standard tools and techniques.

Electrical System Features. The ignition of a chain saw is a simple combination of magneto, spark plug, and breaker points. A pull of the starter cord spins a magnet to generate a surge of current within a coil. As the points break, a high-voltage discharge across the plug ignites the fuel at the correct instant.

Two improvements in this system are *electric starting* and *solid-state ignition*. Electric starting eliminates the rope pull and makes starting, as in the family car, automatic. Engine cranking is done by a small electric motor inside the saw. After the engine is running, the starter motor stops drawing current from the battery. Now the starter motor is converted to an electrical generator and charges the battery for the next start.

Solid-state ignition reduces electric current flow and wear at the breaker points and improves ignition performance. Both the self-starting and the solid-state ignition features improve safety when attempting restart while you're up a tree, but they significantly increase a chain saw's cost.

CHOOSING A CHAIN SAW

Start by browsing among the special features just described. Some features may be outright necessities for you; others may be a matter of convenience, but worth the extra cost. Part of the decision depends on how often you expect to use the tool and on what sort of work. A tree surgeon might find a self-starter indispensable, but it's hardly crucial for the weekend cutter. Once you've selected the features you think are essential, judge the saw's basic attributes. Merely picking one up and moving it about will tell you if the manufacturer has located the handles with careful regard to the machine's center of gravity; a well-balanced tool is less tiresome to hold and safer to manipulate. Determine if the controls are convenient to reach—especially the on-off switch. You must be able to kill the engine instantly in a moment of danger. The handles should have some kind of vibration-damping provision, either rubber or plastic, or else your hands may develop red spots or tingle after a sawing session. Handles

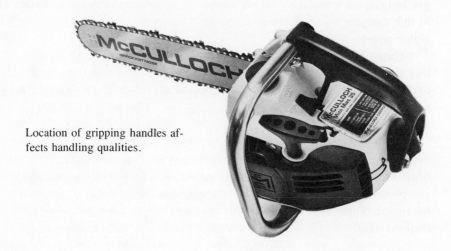

Location of gripping handles affects handling qualities.

should also be ribbed for a firm, non-skid grip to prevent the tool from slipping away.

Take a close look at what the manufacturer has done to ease maintenance. Is the air cleaner easily removed for servicing? Can you tighten the chain, reach the spark plug, and get to the carburetor or other serviceable items without disassembling half the saw?

The final choice of size and power must be left to the individual buyer, but consider the approximate capacities that seem to satisfy most amateurs for jobs around the yard. The single most important dimension is the length, or cutting capacity, of the guide bar. The length of the cutting bar is an important specification in choosing a chain saw. Ranging in size from about 10 to 60 inches, the bar determines the saw's cutting capacity: a saw could cut *twice* the length of the bar. You can cut, for example, from *both* sides of a tree. The longer the bar, the more costly the saw because of higher power and weight. In larger sizes, too, the bar may require the added complexity of a *gear drive*. Such models, however, are not for the amateur; they are too massive and powerful for casual use.

The largest-size bar a homeowner or other occasional user might need is 16 inches; popular sizes fall in the 12- to 14-inch class. A bar that's too large limits your agility in tight places, and the saw will be too heavy for easy one-hand trimming. Many weekend users purchase saws in the standard "6-pound" category. (To this figure must be added, however, the weight of the bar and of gas and oil, for a total of nearly 9 pounds.) The suburbanite would find a saw in this category easier to hold while atop a ladder than a huskier model of higher power.

Chain saw engines are usually rated in cubic inches of displacement rather than horsepower. Engine sizes range to 9 cubic inches, but the amateur should find saws in the 2- to 3-inch range sufficiently powerful. The manufacturer matches the size of the cutting bar to engine power, so the buyer doesn't have to worry about this consideration.

Quality of construction varies in chain saws, and it may be apparent to the buyer's eye. Paying for heavy-duty construction may not be justified if the saw is used for a total cutting time of only a dozen or so hours per year. In this case you probably won't need costly ball bearings, extra-rugged design, or a powerful engine. These are important only if the saw will be used in continuous, arduous cutting.

HOW TO USE A CHAIN SAW

Before you begin cutting, consider carefully the preliminary steps detailed by the manufacturer. He'll specify exact amounts of oil and fuel to be mixed—not inside the chain saw tank but in a separate container. Whenever fuel is replenished, fill the oil tank that lubricates the chain as well. Special oil is available for the purpose, but some manufacturers allow SAE No. 30 motor oil. The instructions may suggest that a pint of kerosene be added to each quart of oil to keep the mixture flowing freely in cold weather. (Kerosene also helps to keep the chain free of sap and pitch in any season.) With manual oiling you should press the button before each cut—and more frequently when cutting through logs of more than about 6 inches.

Proper chain tension is important. If the chain is loose it can jump out of the cutting bar and break. Too much tautness, and the chain wears out rapidly. Turn the adjusting screws or nuts until the chain fits snugly around the bar but can still be moved by hand. Caution: wear gloves or cover the cutters with a cloth while checking tension, or you might cut your hands. And never adjust chain tension while the engine is running. If the saw is new, expect the chain to loosen and need frequent retensioning during the first few hours of use.

A word about chain breakage: many people fear a dangerous whipping action from a chain that breaks while the saw is in operation. There is no hazard here. Rather than flying through the air, a broken chain falls limply to the ground.

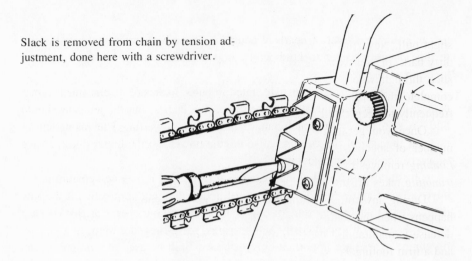

Slack is removed from chain by tension adjustment, done here with a screwdriver.

After the saw is adjusted and fueled, the usual starting procedure is to turn on the ignition switch and apply partial throttle. Use the choke when the engine is either cold or extremely hot. For a cold engine the choke enriches the fuel mixture for easy starting; if the engine is too hot, the choking action sucks out vapors that accumulate in the carburetor.

After a few pulls of the rope the engine starts. Keep the engine running at low speed for a few moments of warm-up. Never turn up the engine to full speed unless the chain is actually contacting wood.

A whirling chain saw is not only a potent cutting tool but a lethal weapon as well. Almost any accident can be avoided by carefully following a few safety rules. Clear away brush or rocks that might cause you to lose footing, and start the saw on a firm surface. Don't, of course, stand under a limb you're cutting. Cut *away* from your body. Be wary of a sapling or other projection that might grab the chain and pull you off balance. When you walk from one cutting area to the next, turn off the saw.

The loud noise of a chain saw engine competes with your alertness, so be conscious of some special hazards. If someone tries to warn you his words may be drowned out, so turn off your saw immediately if you see someone shouting. Don't make sudden turning movements with the saw in your hand because you may strike someone standing within the arc. Keep bystanders a safe distance from your work area so they won't be struck by falling debris.

The basic cutting technique with a chain saw starts by moving the saw's pivot point (at the underside of the chain) toward the work and revving the engine to full throttle. As the chain bites the material be ready to counteract a slight pull. Never let the chain strike the ground or other obstructions or chew dirty bark, or you will quickly dull the cutters. Not much pressure is needed to slice through wood, so be ready to close the throttle as soon as the cutters complete their pass and break free. Don't forget to press the oiler button frequently to keep chain and guide thoroughly lubricated.

Once you get the feel of a chain saw, you can efficiently perform a number of specialized tasks. *Bucking* is cutting a log into desired lengths. *Limbing* removes branches from a tree that's been cut down, while *pruning* or *trimming* takes off undesired branches of a living tree.

During any cutting operation your saw may occasionally kick back. This happens when the chain catches inside a cut or strikes an obstruction. The best defense is maintaining the recommended grip on the saw, good body balance, and a firm footing.

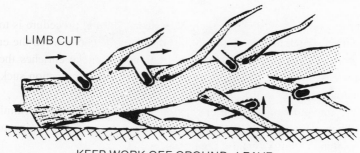

LIMB CUT

KEEP WORK OFF GROUND. LEAVE
SUPPORT LIMBS UNTIL LOG IS CUT

Limbing a fallen tree.

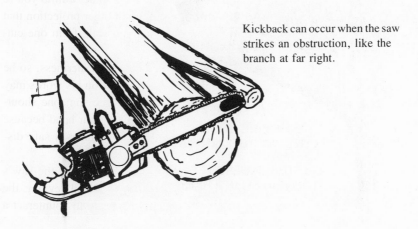

Kickback can occur when the saw strikes an obstruction, like the branch at far right.

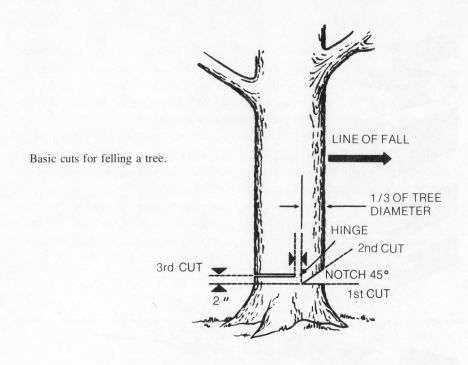

Basic cuts for felling a tree.

LINE OF FALL

1/3 OF TREE DIAMETER

HINGE

2nd CUT

3rd CUT

NOTCH 45°

1st CUT

2 "

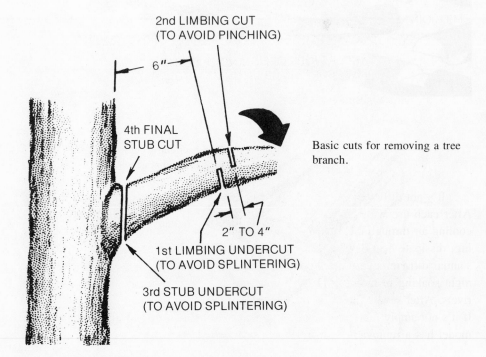

2nd LIMBING CUT
(TO AVOID PINCHING)

6 "

4th FINAL
STUB CUT

Basic cuts for removing a tree branch.

2" TO 4"

1st LIMBING UNDERCUT
(TO AVOID SPLINTERING)

3rd STUB UNDERCUT
(TO AVOID SPLINTERING)

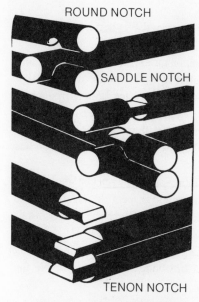

ROUND NOTCH

SADDLE NOTCH

TENON NOTCH

Useful joints in chain saw
carpentry.

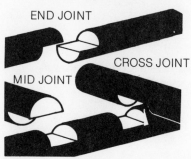

END JOINT

CROSS JOINT

MID JOINT

MAINTAINING THE CHAIN SAW

It's not difficult to keep a chain saw keen and in good running condition. After each use wipe away dirt that could foul the lubrication system or block cooling air through the cylinder fins. (The fins, concealed inside the saw housing, dissipate heat developed by the engine.) If moving parts accumulate substantial dirt, remove the chain completely and wash it in kerosene. An overnight soaking in motor oil allows lubricant to penetrate deeply into the chain rivets. After several hours of chain saw operation, check the sprocket bearing. If it's not amply lubricated, clean and repack it with waterproof grease. If your model has a removable exhaust stack, occasionally detach it and scrape away carbon deposits (but don't let carbon bits fall into the cylinder through the exhaust port).

Another vulnerable item is the cutting bar, or guide. Examine it often, and clean the groove and oiling holes of foreign matter with a piece of wire. Blue discolorations are a clue that you're not pressing the oiler button frequently enough or that the chain is dull. A bar's life is extended by reversing it on its mounting; but check the wear patterns, shown in the illustration. They may indicate it's time to replace the bar. Also look the saw over to see if vibration has loosened nuts, bolts, or other parts.

If your engine, while running, expires for no apparent reason, the trouble could be a clogged air filter. Periodically remove and inspect the air filter to be sure it's absolutely clean and not blocking the air flow. Wash the filter in fuel, blow it clean, and let it dry before replacing.

Another item that wears with use is the spark plug. When engine starting is difficult, or if the plug has been in service for about 20 hours, remove the

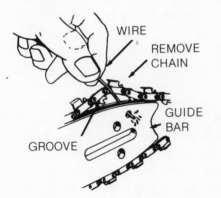

Oiler hole in cutting bar is cleaned with wire to remove chips and sawdust.

Crooked cuts are caused by uneven wear in cutting-bar rails.

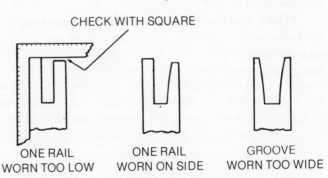

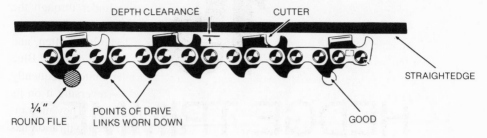

Major resharpening points on chain: drive links, cutters, and depth gauges.

plug with a wrench and clean the electrodes with emery paper or very fine sandpaper. Briskly blow any particles from the working end of the plug. Use a gauge to keep the gap (about .025 inch, usually specified as ''25 thousandths'') at the manufacturer's recommended width. Wipe the porcelain insulator clean with a rag to prevent high-voltage arc-overs. Only if you have faith in your mechanical ability, and a thorough set of service instructions, should you attempt to adjust the carburetor. It's a precise instrument that may need a professional's touch.

Sharpening the chain is another chore. You'll know it's time when sawdust no longer emerges as chips but as a fine powder. A dull saw also demands more manual pressure to cut through wood. Although many owners prefer to have sharpening done by a professional, most manufacturers offer special accessories that enable the novice to do a reasonably good job. One is a special holder, or guide, that positions a round file at exactly the correct angle to create a new cutter edge. After cutters have been resharpened two or three times, another filing operation is done on the chain's *depth gauges,* which control the depth of the saw cut. This job is also simplified by using a special metal guide available from your dealer.

Finally, don't store a chain saw for a long period without first operating the engine until it consumes the fuel remaining in the carburetor. Drain the oil tank and remove the chain and bar. These last two items won't deteriorate in storage if you first wrap them in a cloth soaked with oil.

15
HEDGE TRIMMER

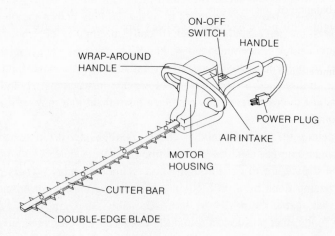

Quick popularity for the electric hedge trimmer was almost inevitable. Operating hand shears is a tiring, blistering chore that takes many hours on a heavily planted lot. The electrified version does the job about six times as fast and neater. It trims hedges, shrubs, and bushes and does small-branch pruning.

THE BASIC HEDGE TRIMMER

Most trimmers contain an electric motor within a housing that elongates into a handle. A power cord emerging from the handle carries ordinary house current at about 300 to 400 watts. If the model is cordless it consumes power from rechargeable batteries contained within the motor housing or in a separate power pack. The motor's rotary motion is converted into reciprocal action for driving a cutter assembly back and forth.

In the simplest cutter design a single-edge blade moves back and forth over a fixed bar. A double-edge model deploys the cutting edge along both sides of the bar. In models with *reciprocating* blades there is no fixed bar; the two halves of the cutter move back and forth. Depending on the model, blades move from 2000 to 3600 strokes per minute on a bar that may extend from 12 to 22 inches.

HOW TO CHOOSE A HEDGE TRIMMER

The balance of the machine is important because your arms bear the trimmer's weight. Grasp the handles and check that they are strategically located;

Electric trimmer cuts about six times as fast as hand shearing.

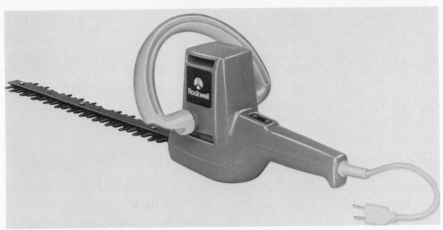
Wrap-around handle is versatile grip.

the tool will be less tiring to use, especially if it falls in the heavier-weight class (over 6 or 7 pounds). There is usually a handle molded into the motor housing, and a second grip farther forward. The forward handle often can be mounted on either side of the housing to agree with your handedness. This option isn't necessary in models with a wrap-around handle, which can be gripped at both sides and also at the top—a convenient position for certain tool operations.

An ideal trimmer cuts through stems up to about ¼ inch thick and needs few repeat passes to level a given area. This is where the model with a double cutting edge is superior: if stubborn stems protrude after the first pass, you can easily reverse the sweep for a second chance with the back of the cutter. This procedure is more difficult using a single-edge model. Blade shape also affects cutting action; thick hedges fall more easily under a trimmer with wide spaces (up to about 1 inch) between the teeth.

Blade length is another consideration. A short blade of about 12 inches is satisfactory for light shrubbery but difficult to handle on big jobs. When cutting a wide hedge, for example, a short blade may not reach stems on the far side, compelling you to walk around to the other side of the hedge. Sometimes you may not have access to the other side—when the hedge backs up on a fence, building, or other obstruction, for example—and here a longer blade length will be definitely preferable.

For operating a trimmer you'll need a long extension cable. The cord limits your mobility and is one more item to be wary about cutting accidentally. This makes a cordless trimmer seem appealing—there is total freedom and no shock hazard. A cordless model, however, needs considerable attention. Generally the batteries operate for about 1 hour, then require about 12 hours of charge. Further, the batteries must not be allowed to lose their charge during long periods of inactivity, as in wintertime storage. Sometimes batteries require "conditioning," a series of discharge-charge cycles to bring the system to full capacity. Weigh these factors to determine whether eliminating the power cord is worth the added maintenance of a cordless model.

When looking for an extension cord to operate an electric trimmer, consider cords especially made for the purpose. Labeled for outdoor use, they come in 50- and 100-foot length. These cords are colored orange or yellow to stand out in bright contrast against a green natural background. If your trimmer has double insulation choose a 2-conductor extension cord, which usually has No. 16 wires; trimmers with a 3-wire system call for a 3-conductor extension cord. One handy accessory that keeps the cord firmly attached to the trimmer plug as you move about is a special connector with slots to hold plug and socket together.

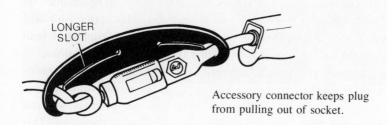

LONGER SLOT

Accessory connector keeps plug from pulling out of socket.

Other details to consider in a trimmer are switch location and ease of brush replacement. Safety is enhanced if the on-off switch is within instant reach or, better yet, has a spring return that must be continuously held down for the motor to function. In this case if you stumble or lose your grip on the tool the power automatically turns off.

Another special feature on some models is a small pruning saw at the tip of the tool. It cuts through thicker stems than can the trimmer's regular cutting edges.

HOW TO USE A HEDGE TRIMMER

Before you turn on the tool, try this trick to keep from slicing the cord as you cut a swath through the hedge. Pass the cord across your shoulders and behind your neck. Lead one end of it over your shoulder and along the inside of

Note dangerous position of power cord, looping just above cutters.

your right arm, and the other end under your left arm. This drapes the cord behind you well away from the furiously cutting blade. Allow a bit of slack where the cord enters the tool so you can swing your arms without drawing the cord around your shoulders.

A safe technique with a trimmer is to grip both handles as you cut. Besides affording good support, it discourages the dangerous habit of grasping the stem you're cutting. If the blade should ever jam, turn off the power and

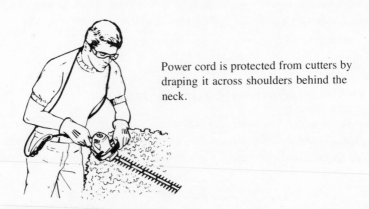

Power cord is protected from cutters by draping it across shoulders behind the neck.

Temporary guideline helps the beginner obtain an accurate cut.

remove the plug before trying to extract the impacted stem. Cutter edges are sharp, so save your fingers by clearing the teeth with a short stick.

A sure sign of well-kept property is a neat hedge, cut with precision. It takes practice to achieve expertise with a trimmer, but good results are not difficult after a couple of trials. For the first attempt erect a simple guideline to follow. A string stretched across the hedge is one possibility—but work carefully because the trimmer could easily cut it. An alternative is a thin strip of wood supported horizontally across upright stakes and leaned against the hedge. With practice your eye soon improves and guidelines become unnecessary.

Use a wide, sweeping motion on light or new growth. If you miss any stems, clip them on a second pass. Best results occur by tilting the blade slightly down into the hedge in the direction you're moving. When attacking thick twigs the technique is slightly different. Move your hands back and forth, as if you're sawing, to improve the feed and to clear the blades of debris. You will soon be able to judge the exact combination of sweeping and sawing to cope with different growths—slowing the feed to negotiate a thick twig, or angling the blade to cut just a few branches at a time. Don't load the motor so much as to slow it down.

If you don't know the fundamentals of hedge trimming, start with this general approach, followed by many gardeners. Keep the approximate height of a hedge to about 5 feet or less. The hedge should be no more than about 30 inches wide (unless you have a screening or other protective function in mind). A hedge may develop spindly foliage if you cut its sides perfectly straight because the lower areas won't receive enough sunlight. This problem is avoided by gently tapering the sides toward the top of the hedge. The narrower top results in less shading below and promotes better growth. Another advan-

Tilt the blade slightly down, into hedge.

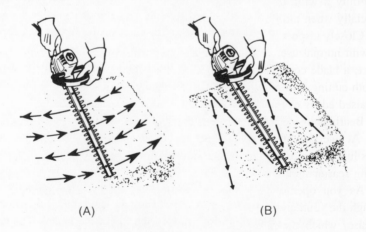

(A)   (B)

Trim new growth (A) with a sweeping motion. Heavy growth (B) is
trimmed with a sawing motion.

Trimmer can slide under fence to reach difficult areas.

tage of a broad-base hedge is improved resistance to the weight of heavy snow. To cut the sides, begin near the bottom and sweep the trimmer blade upward at a slight slant toward the top.

You can also use a hedge trimmer to clip patches of grass that can't be reached by a lawn mower. Sweep the trimmer blade under a fence or around an obstruction in a back-and-forth motion.

MAINTAINING THE HEDGE TRIMMER

After a cutting session the blade may be covered with plant mash or sap. Remove the power plug and, without wetting the motor housing, remove debris with a rag or brush dipped in water. Dry the blades thoroughly with a cloth, then protect them against tarnish with a light film of oil wiped on with a rag. Some blades have a low-friction coating that resists dirt and corrosion, and need only a wipe to keep clean. Even these can be lightly oiled, however, especially when the trimmer is being stored for the winter.

Closely inspect the blades occasionally. Most blades don't need resharpening with normal use. If you strike a stone, wire, piece of glass, or other hard object, a blade could sustain a nick. So long as the nick doesn't interfere with smooth cutting action, leave it alone. If rubbing occurs against the bar, remove the raised edges of the nick with a fine file or sharpening stone.

Bearings inside many trimmers are self-lubricating and don't require attention. At one end of the motor housing in some models, though, is a bearing that's lubricated through an oiling hole. A few drops of machine oil twice each cutting season should take care of it.

As you operate the trimmer, you may notice sparking at the brushes through the ventilation slots in the housing. After a few years the sparking may increase, which means that the brushes are probably ready for replacement. Follow the manufacturer's suggestion—replace brushes through their access caps, or take the tool to a local service center.

16
ROTARY LAWN MOWER

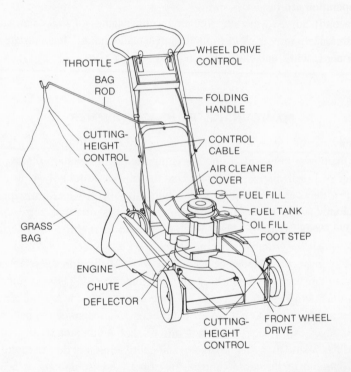

THROTTLE

WHEEL DRIVE CONTROL

BAG ROD

FOLDING HANDLE

CUTTING-HEIGHT CONTROL

CONTROL CABLE

AIR CLEANER COVER

FUEL FILL

FUEL TANK

OIL FILL

FOOT STEP

GRASS BAG

ENGINE

CHUTE DEFLECTOR

CUTTING-HEIGHT CONTROL

FRONT WHEEL DRIVE

There are many ways to cut a lawn. You can ride, walk, push, or be pulled. There's a choice of power source, too—gasoline, house current, or batteries. But if you follow the national pattern in lawn mower selection, the statistics say that 9 to 1 you will buy a gas-powered rotary. This is the walk-behind model with a horizontal blade whirling within a flat metal housing.

Other mowers are either too specialized or too expensive for most home-owners. There is the riding model—a mechanical bronco that cuts a yard-wide swath with little more operator effort than turning a steering wheel. With its high price tag, the riding mower is most practical for estate-size lots of a half acre or more, or when ordinary mowing is prohibited for health reasons. Or you might justify the high cost of a riding mower by the fact that it also takes attachments for snow removal in winter. It can be fitted with accessories for seeding, spreading fertilizer, and removing lawn debris as well.

Starting a gas-engine lawn mower once demanded considerable muscle and profanity, so the electric mower appeared. Its appeal is due to a tiny toggle switch: just flick it on, and the motor hums to life and runs as long as there is electricity from the nearby house. Despite this advantage, as well as that of quieter operation, the electric mower hasn't carved much of a niche in the marketplace. It has two drawbacks. It is a light-duty machine that develops only a fraction of the power released by a small gas engine; and it needs a long extension cord, with careful attention by the operator to avoid running over it.

Electric lawn mower. Note the power
cord emerging from handle at top.

The cord is eliminated in battery-powered mowers, but again there is an inherent power limit, which shows up when the cutting gets tough. A battery-powered mower also needs considerable recharging. For these reasons the gasoline engine dominates the field.

Regardless of power source, mowers are either *rotary* or *reel* in type. Before the heyday of the power mower, when machines were driven by hand, lawn mowers were of the reel type. In this case a cylinder of curving blades turns against a fixed knife. By adding a gas engine to drive the blades, the effort needed to push a reel mower is slashed. The greatest advantage of the reel design is that it does a most effective job on short grasses. A lawn with a manicured appearance is apt to have been mowed with a machine of this type. If you want your lawn to resemble a fine putting green and are willing to put in the time and effort to do the grooming, a reel mower may be your choice. Market statistics, however, show that not many people buy the reel mower—fewer than 10 percent.

The rotary mower captivates most buyers for good reason. It has a prodigious ability to roll into tall grass and tough weeds and leave in its wake growth no higher than an inch or two. The rotary threshes through vegetation that would stymie a reel mower. Because of its blade design a rotary also trims closer to trees, shrubs, and other vertical obstacles. And it's quickly set up to mulch leaves, too. To complete its appeal, the rotary mower needs fewer blade adjustments than does a reel mower. When a rotary blade dulls, it is easily sharpened at home.

The rotary, however, has certain shortcomings. It can be a dangerous implement if you don't follow the operating rules carefully. During the early nineteen-seventies, in an effort to set standards to reduce operating hazards, there were many technical improvements. The chief danger is from the rotating blade—it can pick up stones, nails, and other debris and hurl them out of the mower with formidable force. Another danger is accidentally putting fingers or toes under the mower near the blade. Great strides, however, have been made in lowering the risk—if you select a well-designed model.

THE BASIC ROTARY LAWN MOWER

The heart of a rotary mower is its propellor-like blade, nearly 2 feet in diameter, which spins at high velocity. Reaching a tip speed as great as 19,000 feet per minute, it exerts a powerful suction that erects the grass under the housing. Depth of cut is adjusted by raising or lowering the mower wheels.

Cut-off matter circulating inside the housing is dispensed in two ways. Some of the debris remains trapped inside, filtering down into the lawn to serve as mulch. Most of the trimmings, however, are forced under pressure through a discharge opening in the mower housing to the outside or into a grass-catching bag.

Driving force behind the blade is supplied in most models by a one-cylinder gas engine of 3 to 4 hp. A few 2-stroke engines are sold but the 4-stroke design is far more common. It runs on regular gasoline and has a separate crankcase for lubricating oil. In the 2-stroke engine gas and oil are pre-mixed, and the oil is consumed by combustion as it lubricates. Oil in the 4-stroke engine recirculates.

To avoid the difficulty in starting that characterized bygone engines, many current models have an improved carburetor. They are often self-priming—which introduces an extra charge of fuel into the cylinder for starting. An automatic choke also enriches the mixture to help fire a cold engine. Once the engine is running, a tank of 1- to 2-quart capacity fuels the mower without refilling over all but the most extensive areas.

In a self-propelled mower, engine power is delivered to a transmission (whose square case is seen at lower right) that turns front wheels.

The controls of a mower are straightforward. Although engineers have contrived a number of different starting systems, the winner is still the simple rope pull. It's jerked to crank the engine, then allowed to recoil gently back into the top of the motor housing. Engine speed is controlled by a throttle, usually within easy reach on the mower handle. If a mower is self-propelled (as described below), part of the engine power is delivered to the wheels to reduce pushing effort. A wheel drive control engages a transmission, which propels either front or back wheels over the ground.

SPECIAL FEATURES

An engine is easier to start with *compression release,* which means that a valve releases part of the pressure built up in the cylinder as you pull the rope, thereby reducing starting effort by about one half. Most effortless of all is *electric start.* As in an automobile you merely turn a key, whereupon a battery-powered starter motor cranks the gas engine. The battery, which retains enough energy for 70 or more starts—enough for a typical mowing season—is restored by a charger plugged into house current. This is a costly feature, but one that may be justified if you frequently stop the engine to empty a grass bag or change attachments, for example.

Another effort-cutting improvement is a *self-propelling* feature. Using power take-off from the engine, the wheels advance over the ground as you gently direct the action. This feature is desirable for large areas or for uneven terrain that would demand considerable exertion with a conventional mower. If your lawn has many small mowing areas, however, requiring repeated back-ups and turn-arounds, a hand-pushed power mower may be easier to manipulate. Another way to reduce pushing effort is to buy a mower with an aluminum or magnesium housing. These materials reduce housing weight by nearly one half compared with common steel construction. They are also more immune to rusting than steel; but they're more likely to crack if struck a moderate blow.

Other features you'll encounter are a handle that folds for storage or transport, a gas gauge, and a muffler that exhausts through the mower housing for quieter operation. Some models have a wash-out plug at the top of the housing. After a mowing session you can remove the plug and direct a stream of water from a garden hose through the housing while running the engine, to flush out grass clippings and other debris.

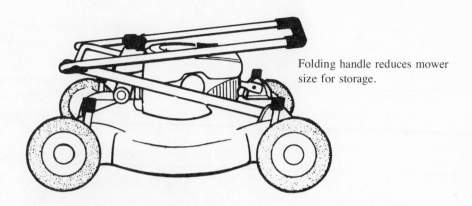

Folding handle reduces mower size for storage.

CHOOSING A ROTARY LAWN MOWER

Look for the Outdoor Power Equipment Institute (OPEI) seal on a mower for reasonable assurance that the machine meets basic safety standards. Even with this seal, however, the mower warrants close inspection. Most important is how the housing enshrouds the blade. It should overhang and extend below the blade tips to reduce chance of injury to a toe or finger.

Another dangerous area is the discharge opening, where trimmings are ejected. The problem here is that hard material—stones, metal items, etc.—lying on the lawn are likely to be picked up and launched out of the opening. For protection from these dangerous projectiles many mowers have a spring-loaded deflecting plate that directs the exhaust stream downward before it emerges from the housing. The plate prevents a foot from entering the opening. The spring mechanism allows the plate to swing open for an attachment like a grass-catching bag, but snaps back when the bag is removed.

Next examine how the grass-catching bag (if there is one) is attached. In some models you must first remove the deflecting plate from the discharge opening. While the grass bag is over the opening there is no hazard because the bag traps foreign objects picked up by the mower. Unless you purchase a mower with an adjustable plate that automatically springs back to cover the hole, be sure to reinstall the deflecting plate when the grass bag is not in use.

The trend is to mount a grass catcher at the rear of the mower. This eliminates a large bulge at the side so that the machine can enter narrower areas or move closer to a vertical obstruction, such as a wall or fence, for flush trimming. A typical model can trim to within 5 or 6 inches of a tree or wall. If your

Grass bag (at left) is attached to discharge chute to contain lawn clippings.

Mower is more maneuverable when grass bag is mounted at rear, not side.

mowing area is large, consider a mower that holds a large-size grass catcher to reduce the number of times you'll have to empty debris. Some bags have a zipper to speed the emptying job.

Other factors affect the maneuverability needed for intricate gardens or tight spaces. Grasp the handle and see if it's comfortable for your height, or has an adjustment to obtain a suitable setting. While checking, push the handle as far forward as it will go. Does it rise so high that your feet can poke dangerously under the rear housing? To help prevent this possibility the rear edge of the housing should have a movable or hinged shield, which also prevents hard objects from exiting to the rear. The shield shouldn't interfere with back-and-forth motion of the mower.

When you've located a machine that satisfies these safety (and personal) requirements, consider horsepower. Two typical mowers have a 3-hp engine and a cutting width of 19 inches, and a 4-hp engine with a 21-inch cut. The significant difference between these models is in how fast they do the job; the larger blade finishes the lawn about 10 percent faster. Cutting height (the height of the clipped grass) is generally adjustable from about 1 to 3 inches by raising or lowering the wheels. Look at the raising mechanism for operating convenience and accessibility. Increasingly manufacturers are stating the engine's *displacement* in cubic inches instead of its horsepower. A 10-cubic-inch engine, for example, is comparable to a 4-hp model.

Other controls deserve scrutiny. Is the throttle within easy reach? The starter pull handle should not compel you to stand in front of the discharge opening when cranking the engine. Also, you'll tire quickly if the direction of pull requires a straining movement of your arm. Is it easy to check the oil, and to drain it from the crankcase at the end of the season?

ACCESSORIES

If a mower doesn't include certain items as original equipment, they can usually be purchased optionally. One is a *mulcher* attachment to contain trimmings within the housing and deposit them evenly on a newly seeded lawn. A *bagging kit* is a good choice, too, if the machine has no grass-catching arrangement. When lawn cuttings are permitted to form a heavy layer, they can smother the grass or prevent moisture and fertilizer from penetrating to the roots.

HOW TO USE A ROTARY LAWN MOWER

A good time to mow is late afternoon or early evening—the newly cut grass can more easily adjust to the shock during the hours after dark. If you're a stickler for perfection, try not to walk on the grass just before cutting so that it will be upright for uniform clipping. After the machine is running, keep children, dogs, and onlookers well away from the discharge opening.

You can choose your own mowing pattern, but one simple approach is to mow around the border of the lawn twice to form a swath about $3^1/_2$ feet wide (two mower widths). Then cross the lawn repeatedly, mowing back and forth in straight lines. Slightly overlap each swath to avoid a ragged appearance. The throttle gives a choice of blade speeds; try an intermediate position for normal cutting. When there's rough going or if you have a grass catcher attached, open the throttle to the full-power setting. As you arrive at the end of a straight run, turn the mower by pressing down on the handle to raise the front wheels and rotating the machine to the new direction on its rear wheels. Be careful not to slip on sloping terrain. A good technique for sure footing is to mow parallel to the slope.

If you mow frequently, you won't have to bother with a grass catcher because short trimmings will probably not affect the lawn. A rule-of-thumb is to schedule your sessions so that no more than about one third of the grass height is removed. In many areas this amounts to twice a week in late spring and early summer. Your lawn will look better if you avoid traveling the same route in successive mowing sessions. Varying the course prevents the grass from growing or lying in one direction only.

MAINTAINING THE ROTARY LAWN MOWER

Immediately after mowing, clean the inside of the housing to rid it of matted or clinging debris; wipe away visible grease and oil. To eliminate any chance of the motor starting while your hands are near the blade, remove the wire from the top of the spark plug. (Be sure the disconnected wire can't spring back to the plug—a spark can jump the small air gap and fire the plug.)

The modest maintenance required for a lawn mower may be done almost entirely at home. If you sense excessive vibration check for loose parts. Vibration may also be caused by an unbalanced blade. It's easy to replace the blade, which is simply unbolted from the engine shaft. If you suspect the blade has

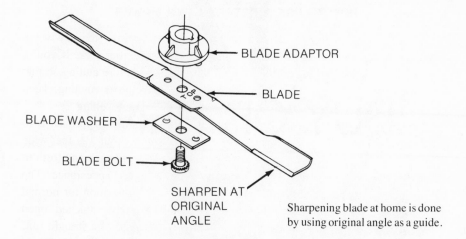

BLADE ADAPTOR

BLADE

BLADE WASHER

BLADE BOLT

SHARPEN AT ORIGINAL ANGLE

Sharpening blade at home is done by using original angle as a guide.

dulled, the lawn's shredded appearance should confirm it. This is another job within reach of most handy owners. With a file made for the purpose, sharpen the blade by following the original angle cut of the manufacturer. To avoid unbalancing the blade in the sharpening process, file the same amount of metal from each cutting edge of the blade.

Hard starting is often caused by a bad spark plug or dirty air cleaner. Purchase an inexpensive plug-gapping tool and check the plug's electrodes for spacing, dirt, and wear after every 25 hours of operation. The plug should be replaced if the outer electrode appears thin and pitted. The air cleaner should be checked occasionally for clogging by dust and foreign matter. Most modern air filters can be cleaned in detergent and water, then squeezed and dried thoroughly. Then oil the cleaner with about five teaspoons of unused engine oil worked uniformly through the spongy material. Other problems, such as a leaking gear case, should be handled by a service center—but first try tightening external nuts and bolts.

17

BUY OR RENT?

More than 10,000 stores around the United States, doing about $2 billion worth of business each year, are a sure sign of a "rental revolution." Although the trend was started by big corporations and building contractors, the householder has helped to make equipment rental a booming industry. Why buy a $300 sander, goes the argument, when it can be rented for $6 a day? A single day may be all you need to refinish your floors.

Nearly any power tool can be rented. According to a survey conducted by the American Rental Association, covering the 20 most frequently rented items, you can obtain many of the tools described in this book. Rates vary considerably, but it's estimated that a one-day rental costs about one twentieth to one tenth of the tool's purchase price. For a fee the tool will be delivered and picked up, or your car rigged with a trailer hitch to tow a machine mounted on wheels.

There are other advantages to renting professional-type power tools. The tool is fueled, adjusted, sharpened, and ready to operate. There's no repair or maintenance to worry about, and you won't surrender precious storage space in your home. Rental brings within your reach tools that aren't sold through regular consumer channels—for example, a pneumatic hammer for breaking up pavement, a powerful steam rug cleaner, a bucket loader, a rock drill, a trench digger. With a few rudimentary lessons you may be able to handle them. Many rental outlets are run by "mom-and-pop" franchisees who will willingly help the beginner.

```
EQUIPMENT LISTED IN ORDER OF RENTAL FREQUENCY
        Floor polishers/sanders/shampooers
        Lawn mowers/edgers
        Trailers/trucks
        Sanders
        Tillers
        Roll-away beds
        Paint spray equipment
        Sewer augers
        Chain saws
        Ladders
        Automotive tools
        Electric saws
        Tables/chairs
        Electric hammers
        Wheelchairs
        Wallpaper steamers
        Cement mixers
        Hospital beds
        Plumbing equipment
        Power posthole augers
```

There are, however, some disadvantages to renting. Almost any power tool, even a simple drill, must be operated according to the manufacturer's instructions—and these may be missing with a rental tool. A clerk in the store may give you verbal instructions, but they are rarely as comprehensive as a leaflet or booklet prepared by the manufacturer. To combat this problem the American Rental Association has prepared special instruction sheets for more than 200 different tools and makes these sheets available to its member stores. If you feel unsure about a tool ask for the printed instructions. Also, be sure that any accessories you require are included with the machine.

Renting a tool is especially handy for those jobs that arise infrequently but are difficult, if not impossible, to do by hand. I recall a ceramic-tile cutter I once used in remodeling a bathroom. Before I rented it I broke several tiles while trying to score and separate each piece by hand. The tile cutter did the job with amazing efficiency. On another job, installing an oak floor, a rented flooring nailer positioned and set up each nail, allowing me to complete the project in about two hours. Other rare jobs—removing paint from house siding, steaming off wallpaper, blowing leaves, shooting studs into concrete—are neatly handled by rented machines.

Cement mixer for small jobs, powered by gasoline or electric motor.

Thus the question of whether to buy or rent must be answered individually. If you're a typical homeowner and enjoy working with wood or other materials, most of the basic power tools described in earlier chapters are worth buying. They often repay their price in less than a year and, with reasonable care, last a generation or more. And owning a tool lets you learn to operate it with more skill and sophistication than is possible with a rented item. When it comes to backhoes or cement mixers, however, rental is far more sensible. About a half dozen tools fall somewhere between the two categories: items that would be nice to own, but that are more practical to rent unless you can justify their cost. Let's look at some of these.

DISK SANDER-POLISHER

A pad-type sander (see chapter 5) is all a home handyman might need for moderate or fine sanding. To do occasional rough sanding when needed, however, a disk sander can supply extra power. It is not intended for finishing—the spinning disk removes material at too rapid a rate. The disk, which is most

Disk sander.

commonly 7 inches in diameter, is flexible and can be applied to rounded contours. This machine is especially popular for refinishing boats, sanding window sills, sashes, and casings, and removing paint from house siding.

The disk sander is also widely used for auto body work. It smoothes fiberglass solder patches and those made with other compounds. Fitted with a wire brush, the tool removes rust scale and old finish from metal surfaces.

The disk polisher is almost interchangeable with the disk sander; the difference is in rate of operation. Sanding calls for much higher speeds—about 4000 rpm—while polishing is done at about half that rate. To satisfy both functions there are dual-speed models with, for example, a maximum capacity of 4700 rpm for sanding and a switch to reduce speed to about 2400 rpm for polishing. The disk polisher is commonly used for shining automobile finish and for buffing furniture, cabinets, and countertops.

Operating a disk sander takes a bit of special technique. You can select paper in any of three basic grit categories, depending on the job: coarse for heavy material removal, medium for taking out scratches caused by the coarse grade, and fine for additional smoothing. (Don't expect a disk sander to prepare a surface for a new finish; you'll need a finishing sander for the final step, or you can complete the job by hand.) When you're ready to sand, grip the tool firmly and turn on the power *before* touching the work. There may be an auxiliary handle at either the left or the right for steadying the tool. Don't apply the sanding disk flat to the work surface or the tool will be difficult to control, its cutting action irregular and bumpy. The correct technique is to tilt the disk at an angle to the work and gently lower the disk until it bends. When in position

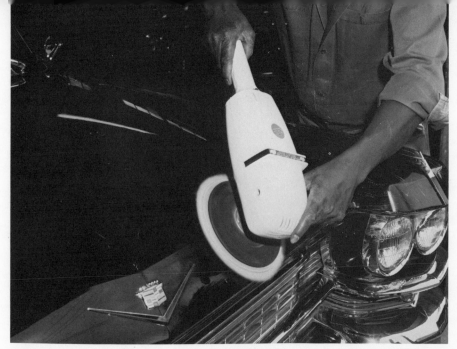

Polisher is used for buffing cars, furniture, cabinets, etc.

only about one third of the disk's surface should be in contact with the work. Avoid tilting at a sharp angle or the edge of the disk may gouge the work.

It takes a nimble hand to get good results with a disk sander. Once you have the right contact angle, move the sander in a long, sweeping swath back and forth, overlapping as you go. Never dwell in a limited area because the instant you stop moving the tool it will eat into the work surface. There is also a temptation to move the machine in a circular motion over the work, but this may cause unsightly swirls.

Two accessories are worth considering if you plan to do specialized jobs with a disk sander. One, an attachment that controls maximum sanding depth, is a good item to install when removing old paint from the exterior of a house. The other attachment is a *feather edger*. It helps prevent severe scratches in the work by a slip clutch action of two pads mounted behind the disk. Exert too much pressure on the tool, and slippage reduces the power.

BELT SANDER

This is the most powerful portable sander an amateur is apt to buy or rent. It can tackle a wide range of smoothing jobs from rough sanding to fine surface finishing. With suitable abrasives, a belt sander also smoothes metal, plastic, stone, and marble.

A typical belt sander contains a motor that drives an endless loop of abrasive around a pair of drums. Power is applied only to the rear drum, which is adjustable by the operator to keep it tracking true at the correct tension. A lever or knob retracts the rear drum to release the belt for changing.

Operating technique follows the basic approach used with most sanders. To avoid gouging or marring the work, turn on the power before touching the abrasive to the work surface, and keep it on until after the machine is lifted away. In many cases the sander should be moved with the grain of the work under no more pressure than the tool's own weight. Keep moving to avoid too much abrasion in one spot and maneuver the machine in long, overlapping strokes. If you want to speed the job, though at some sacrifice of smoothness, cut across the grain or at an angle to it.

The finest finish is achieved if you take down the surface in three progressive steps with abrasive belts in the coarse, medium, and fine categories; move with the grain. If the tool approaches the end of a board, don't let the belt tilt over it or you may get a rounded edge.

Most jobs are done with open-coat aluminum oxide paper, but silicone carbide, which is extremely hard, is used for surfacing stone and marble. Metal

Belt sander.

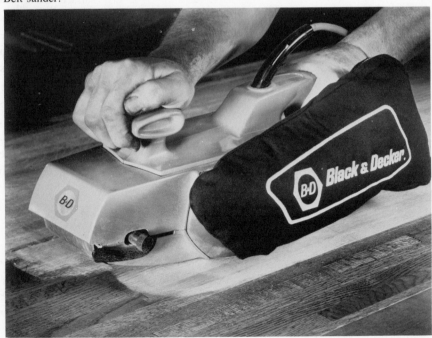

is finished with special belts and a lubricant made for the purpose. Because belt sanders generate much dust, use a dust collector attachment, available for most models.

RECIPROCATING SAW

This is a popular tool among plumbers, carpenters, and electricians. Powerful and rugged, the reciprocating saw makes short shrift of certain cuts that are difficult to accomplish with any other tool. These are mostly "roughing-in" operations—cutting openings in walls, floors, and ceilings for pipes, ducts, and electrical outlets. In old construction the tool rapidly slices through plaster, wallboard sheathing, or siding to add new doors and windows. It's especially useful in making cuts in the tight quarters of an attic or crawl space. Depending on choice of blade, the reciprocating saw cuts through wood, sheet metal, pipe, conduit, or almost any other building material.

This saw is not a good choice for routine wood working. Although it can do some of the same work as a circular or saber saw, it's really intended for rough cutting. It's also an expensive investment, owing to its powerful motor and tough casing intended to stand the physical abuse of construction work. These factors make the reciprocating saw a good bet for rental rather than purchase. If you want to tackle a major home improvement that requires cutting through the building's basic structure, the tool will save you much effort. Just cutting an opening for a new door in an existing wall is an aggravating, tedious job with most other power tools.

A typical model has a 1-hp motor that drives a blade back and forth at about 2000 strokes per minute. The stroke varies according to the model from about $^3/_4$ to over 1 inch. Some saws have a two-speed switch to control the motor, while others have a variable-speed trigger for smooth control over a continuous speed range. To ensure good cutting action the saw has a shoe near the base of the blade that is applied against the work. The blade usually can be mounted in several positions with respect to the housing, allowing cuts in at least four directions. This feature helps in maneuvering the saw in tight corners.

To operate a reciprocating saw, place the shoe against the work surface to steady the tool. Turn on the power, lower the blade, and draw it along the cutting line. Always shut off the motor *before* lifting the blade from the work to avoid a snag or kickback.

Another valuable capability of this saw is plunge cutting—making an interior cut without starting from the edge of the work. This is essential when making cut-outs in walls, for example. Start the saw, but this time use the shoe as a pivot and angle the moving blade into the work until its cuts completely through.

There's a wide choice of blades to fit the saw, depending on the job. For roughing in, blades run as long as 12 inches. Special types cut through plaster, metal, asbestos, or hard rubber. When cutting metal or other dense material use slow speed and a few drops of SAE No. 30 oil to reduce friction and heat.

The moving blade of a reciprocating saw is not especially dangerous, but there is another hazard. Because the saw often is used to cut into walls there's risk of slicing through a live electrical cable. So long as the saw has its 3-wire cable properly grounded (see page 8), this should only blow a house fuse. Shock hazard is also reduced if the tool has a double-insulated housing. To avoid severing wires, pipes, or ducts, make a small initial opening in the wall and check for obstructions within before plunging the blade deeply into the hole.

IMPACT WRENCH

This is a familiar tool to any carowner used to having a flat tire repaired at a service station. Instead of spinning an X-shaped wrench by hand, the service man applies an impact wrench that speedily removes and installs the wheel nuts. A similar model is also available for home use. Unlike many professional types it needs no compressor or air hoses for power. The tool plugs into an ordinary house current outlet.

Impact wrench quickly removes or installs bolts.

Impact wrench with socket assortment.

An impact wrench can prove a tremendous boon if you're working on a major repair job on a car or other machinery with dozens of nuts and bolts. It's up to 90 percent faster than doing the equivalent work by hand. Besides loosening and tightening nuts, bolts, cap screws, and lag bolts, the impact wrench can remove threaded pieces of hardware that are "frozen" in place.

A typical impact wrench has a $1/3$-hp electric motor that spins an internal striker assembly containing two steel balls. About 2000 blows per minute are transmitted by the striker to an anvil, which holds the socket. The nut or bolt being tightened is turned smoothly until it seats. Then the wrench strikes with rotary motion up to a maximum force of about 125 foot-pounds.

When the tool is operated to tighten a nut, the socket must be squarely placed on the nut and gentle pressure applied; driving a nut at an angle could damage the socket. In a nut-tightening operation a reversing lever is placed in the forward position and the trigger depressed. It takes judgment to know when the bolt is tight and to stop impacting, but it's usually no more than about a half turn after seating. Too much hammering could ruin the thread or cause breakage.

To remove hardware, place the lever in reverse and keep impacting until the item loosens, then spins off freely. Never throw the reversing lever if the machine is still turning in a forward direction. Another precaution: don't use ordinary sockets in an impact tool. You'll need sockets made especially for the purpose, available typically in an assortment of ten ranging in size from $^7/_{16}$ to 1 inch.

WELDER

The searing heat developed in an electrical arc or by burning gases is the key to the art of welding. With a welder you can mend broken metal parts, join wrought iron, build substantial structures of steel tubing or angle iron, fix autos, bicycles, appliances, and tools. A welder softens metal for bending and tempering, or cuts through material that's too hard to saw.

The *arc* welder is driven by electricity. By drawing power through a transformer, the circuit converts line voltage—either 115 or 230 volts—into tremendous amperage of about 180 amps in a moderate-duty model. Even a light welder made for use with ordinary house current (115 volts) may need a 15- to 30-ampere fuse to deliver sufficient power. Thus, if you're considering an arc welder be aware of the current requirements in advance. Most conventional welders demand a 230-volt circuit, which must be installed by an electrician. This circuit is similar to that for an electric range or hot-water heater.

If you rent an arc welder, power may be no problem because, along with the basic equipment, you'll get a gas-engine-driven generator that delivers the necessary current. What's more, you can use the machine outdoors because of its independent power source. This may be an attractive idea if you want to do a considerable amount of iron working—anything from furniture making to sculpting—outside your home. If your needs are less—you merely want to weld a piece broken from a motorcycle, say—the rental fee (quoted at $16 per day at one rental store in 1975) may not be worth it. A local welding shop would probably do the job more cheaply.

Arc welding takes practice but the basic idea is simple. The work is clamped to a steel baseplate, which serves as the electrical ground of the circuit. In your hand is the other electrode, which terminates in a rod. The arc is struck by scratching or tapping the rod against the work. As the arc appears, the tip of the rod is quickly withdrawn about $^1/_8$ inch and the arc is permitted to melt the edges of the metal to be joined. The temperature of 8000 degrees F forms a crater and small pool of molten metal. A flux coating on the welding rod simultaneously burns to form a gas screen around the arc, preventing the molten metal from becoming contaminated by gases in the surrounding air. Part of the rod also melts and flows into the weld, adding mass and strength.

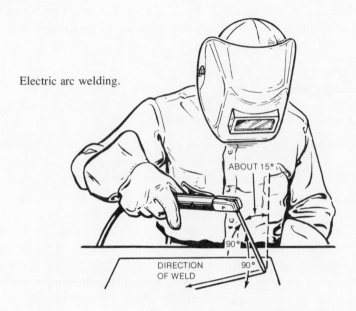

Electric arc welding.

ABOUT 15°

90°

DIRECTION 90°
OF WELD

Another type of welder, the *gas torch*, derives heat from the combustion of oxygen and acetylene. The operator grips an oxyacetylene torch that is connected through rubber hoses to two gas tanks. Inside the torch are adjustable needle valves for each gas, a mixing chamber, and a single passageway to carry the mixture to the tip of the torch for burning. The mixture is varied by the operator until the flame has a clear, well-defined white cone (known as a ''neutral flame''). An incorrect gas mixture wastes fuel or causes poor welding action. Once the torch is applied, it welds by radiant heat melting the metal.

The basic technique with either an arc or a gas welder is the same. As the tool tip is moved along the melting edges of the seam, a rod is fed into the joint to add filler metal. When done along a continuous line this is called *running a bead;* if only every few inches, it's *tack* welding. A sign of a good weld joint is a bead of metal that just covers the seam and displays a rippled appearance.

Which is the preferred welding outfit—gas or electric? Both demand about the same level of skill; and you can operate the tool with its own gas or electricity source, so power is no problem. The gas welder is often the choice for finer work because you can install various tips to change the flame proportions. It's possible, however, to install carbon electrodes on some arc welders to create a heat applicator not unlike that of a gas welder. Instead of running current through the work and a rod, the arc is struck across the two carbon elec-

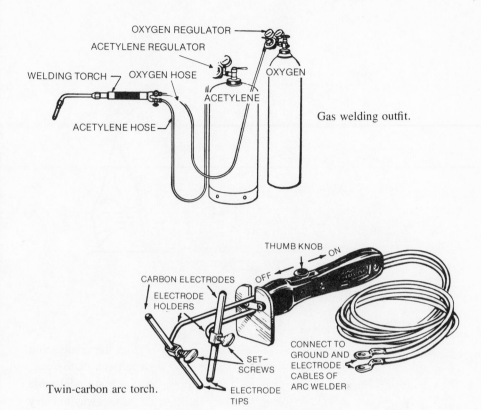

Gas welding outfit.

Twin-carbon arc torch.

trodes. Regardless of welding outfit, be sure to obtain a welder's helmet to protect your eyes from glare and heat. Heavy leather gloves and clothing protect against hot sparks or molten splatters.

Browse through a local rental store and you'll find an interesting variety of heavy tools that can turn a major, once-in-a-while chore into an easy job, often at great savings. Don't rely only on printed lists to see what's stocked in these stores. Inventory often varies, and it's worth an inquiry to locate the tool you need.

APPENDIX

The companies and organizations listed below have provided helpful assistance in supplying many of the illustrations that appear in this book. Many of them will furnish additional information in response to a written request.

American Rental Association, 2920 23rd Avenue, Moline, Ill. 61265
Black & Decker Mfg. Co., Towson, Md. 21204
Clausing Corp., 2019 N. Pitcher St., Kalamazoo, Mich. 49001
Dremel Mfg. Co., P.O. Box 518, Racine, Wis. 53401
Electro Engineering Products, 1801 N. Central Park Ave., Chicago, Ill. 60647
J. B. Foote Foundry Co., P.O. Box 236, Fredericktown, Ohio 43019
Homelite, P.O. Box 134, Port Chester, N.Y. 10573
McCulloch Corp., 6101 West Century Blvd., Los Angeles, Cal. 90045
McGraw-Edison Co. (Portable Electric Tools Div.), 1200 E. State St., Geneva, Ill. 60134
Millers Falls Co., 57 Well St., Greenfield, Mass. 01301
Remington, Desa Industries Inc., 25000 S. Western Ave., Park Forest, Ill. 60466
Rockwell Mfg. Co., 400 N. Lexington Ave., Pittsburgh, Pa. 15208
Sears Roebuck and Co., Sears Tower, Chicago, Ill. 60684
Skil Corp., 5033 N. Elston Ave., Chicago, Ill. 60630
The Stanley Works, New Bern, N.C. 28560
Thor Power Tool Co., 175 N. State St., Aurora, Ill. 60507
Toolkraft, 700 Plainfield St., Chicopee, Mass. 01013
Toro Co., 8111 Lindale Ave. S., Bloomington, Minn. 55420
Unimat, American Edelstaal, Inc., 1 Atwood Ave., Tenafly, N.J. 07670
Weller (The Cooper Group), P.O. Box 728, Apex, N.C. 27502

INDEX

American Rental Association, 212, 213

band saw, 172-180
  blades for, 173-178
  description of, 173-177
  maintenance of, 179-180
  miter gauge, 176, 177
  operation of, 178-179
  rip fence, 177
  safety precautions for, 178
  selection of, 173-177
  sizes of, 173-177
  table for, 175, 176, 177
  uses for, 172-173, 178
bayonet saw, *see* saber saw
belt sander, 216-218
  operation of, 217
bench grinder, 94-101
  accessories for, 96-97
    edge tool grinding attachment, 97
    grinding wheels, 96-97
    pedestal, 97
  adjustable eye shield, 96
  description of, 95
  maintenance of, 99, 100
  operation of, 97, 98, 99
  safety precautions for, 95, 97-98, 99
  selection of, 95-96
  uses for, 94-95, 96-97, 98, 99
  water tray, 96
bench saw, *see* table saw
bits:
  carbide-tipped, 22, 114
  carbon steel, 22
  core box, 113

bits (*cont.*)
  dovetailing, 113
  edge, 113
  grooving, 113
  high-speed, 21
  rabbeting, 113
  straight-sided, 113
  twist, 21-22
  veining, 113
  V-groove, 113
blades:
  alternate set, 47
  for band saw, 172, 177-178
  carbide-tipped, 127
  for circular saw, 56-57
  combination, 56
  cross cut, 56
  flooring, 57
  hard-tooth combination, 127
  hollow-ground, 47
  jeweler, 168
  metal-cutting, 47, 56
  planer, 57, 127
  plywood, 56, 127
  for reciprocating saw, 219
  rip, 56
  for saber saw, 43, 168
  saw set, 47
  for scroll saw, 47, 163-164, 167-168, 169-171
  skiptooth, 177
  Teflon-coated, 48
  tungsten-carbide, 48

cabinet work, 109-121
carpentry, 23, 50-51, 167, 172-179

cement mixer, 214
chain saw, 181-193, 213
  all-position carburetor, 184
  automatic oiling device, 184
  built-in sharpener, 185
  compression release, 184
  cutting bar, 186
  description of, 182-184
  electric starting, 185
  maintenance of, 191-193
  muffler, 184-185
  operation of, 187-189
  power of, 182-183, 184, 187
  safety precautions for, 182, 187, 188-189
  selection of, 185-187
  solid-state ignition, 185
  throttle latch, 184
  uses for, 182, 189, 191
circular saw, 1, 2, 3, 35, 50-64, 123
  accessories for, 57
    rip guide, 57
    saw protractor, 57
  blades for, 56-57
  description of, 51, 52
  double insulation for, 53
  electronic brake, 53
  lock-off button, 53
  maintenance of, 63-64
  operation of, 52, 58-61
  riving knife, 53
  safety precautions for, 51, 53, 58, 63
  selection of, 51, 54-55
  slip clutch system, 53, 58
  uses for, 50-51
cords:
  extension, 8-10, 196-197
  3-wire, 6, 8
cost, 2, 3, 16, 18, 19, 78, 149, 152, 153, 165,
    203, 212, 214

decorative objects, 101, 102, 135-146, 152, 163
disk sander-polisher, 66, 214-216
  feather edger, 216
  operation of, 215-216
do-it-yourself kits, 4
double insulation, 8-9, 19, 53
drill, portable electric, 2, 4, 16-33
  accessories for, 22-27
    drill bit sharpener, 24, 26
    drill stand, 26, 27
    sanding-polishing kit, 22
    speed reduction device, 24
  bearings for, 19
  bits for, 16-17, 21-22, 24
  cost of, 18-19
  description of, 16-17, 18-20
  maintenance of, 32-33
  operation of, 29-32

drill, portable electric (cont.)
  press, 26, 27-29
  safety precautions for, 19, 31-32, 33
  selection of, 17-20, 21
  sizes of, 17-18, 20, 21
  speed of, 17-19
  variable-speed control, 18-19
drill press, 27-29
  size of, 29
  spindle speeds for, 28
dual-action sander, see sander

electrical current for tools, 10-11
electronic work, 79, 88

finishing sander, see sander
flux:
  acid, 84
  rosin, 84
furniture making, 123, 152

garden trimming, 194, 197-201
grinders, see bench grinder; hand-held grinder

hand-held grinder, 95, 101-108
  description of, 100, 101, 104-108
  maintenance of, 102
  operation of, 101
  router attachment, 102
  selection of, 101, 102, 103
  uses for, 101-102, 104-108
hedge trimmer, 194-201
  cord connector, 197
  description of, 194-195
  extension cord for, 196-197
  maintenance of, 201
  operation of, 197-201
  pruning saw feature of, 197
  safety precautions for, 197-198
  selection of, 195-197
home remodeling, 1-3
house appraisals, 1, 2

impact wrench, 219-221
  description of, 220
  safety precautions for, 220-221
  uses for, 220

jig saw, see scroll saw

lathe, 135-147
  accessories for, 141-142
    bed gap, 138
    faceplate, 142, 145
    work arbor, 142
  chisels for, 141-142
  description of, 136-138
  faceplate turning, 136, 142, 145-146

lathe (*cont.*)
  maintenance of, 147
  operation of, 142-146
  outboard turning, 141
  selection of, 138-141
  size of, 138-139
  spindles, 136-139
  spindle turning, 136, 140, 143
  types of, 138-141
  uses for, 135, 138
lawn mower, *see* rotary lawn mower

maintenance (*see also* under individual tools), 2,
  6, 11-13
metal work, 27-28, 31, 34, 42-43, 48, 76, 78-89,
  90-92, 167, 168, 171, 178, 221

National Electrical Code, 8

orbital sander, *see* sander
Outdoor Power Equipment Institute (OPEI), 207

pad sander, *see* sander
pencil iron, *see* soldering iron
power tool industry, 3-5
Power Tool Institute (PTI), 5-7
power tools, uses for, 2-4
propane torch, 90-93
  accessories for, 91
    flame spreader, 91
    pencil burner, 91
    soldering tip, 84-86, 91
    spark lighter, 91
    utility burner, 91
  description of, 90-91
  maintenance of, 93
  operation of, 92-93
  safety precautions for, 91
  types of, 90-91

radial arm saw, 51, 122-134, 149
  accessories for, 126-128
    dado set, 127
    disk sander, 128
    drum sander, 128
    molding cutter head, 128
    open frame stand, 127
    rotary planer, 128
    router bit, 128
    sawdust collector, 128
  anti-kickback device, 124, 125
  blade brake, 125
  blades for, 126-127
  description of, 122-123, 124-125
  maintenance of, 133-134
  operation of, 125, 128-133
  safety precautions for, 125, 126
  sawdust spout, 125

radial arm saw (*cont.*)
  selection of, 125-126
  uses for, 122-123
  vacuum connection, 125
reciprocating saw, 218-219
  blades for, 219
  description of, 218
  operation of, 218-219
  safety precautions for, 219
  uses for, 218
rental of tools, 212-214
rotary lawn mower, 202-211, 213
  accessories for, 209
    bagging kit, 209
    mulcher, 209
  automatic choke, 205
  charger, 206
  compression release, 206
  cost, 203
  description of, 203, 204, 205-206
  electric starting, 206
  gas gauge, 206
  grass-catching bag, 207, 208
  maintenance of, 210-211
  muffler for, 206
  operation of, 210
  safety precautions for, 204, 207, 210-211
  selection of, 207-209
  self-propelling feature, 206
  uses of, 204
  wash-out plug, 206
router, 109-121
  accessories, 114-115
    edge guide, 114, 118
    lettering template set, 114, 121
    table, 114-115
  bits, 112-114, 119
  description of, 110-112
  maintenance of, 121
  operation of, 115-121
  safety precautions for, 115
  selection of, 112
  silicone carbide hone, 121
  speed, 112
  uses for, 109-110, 112-113

saber saw, 2, 12, 34-49, 50, 51, 61, 123
  blades for, 42-43, 44, 46-48
  description of, 34-36
  maintenance of, 48-49
  operation of, 42, 43, 45, 46-47
  orbital action, 39
  safety precautions for, 39, 42, 44
  sawdust blower, 39
  scrolling feature, 39
  selection of, 39-42
  sliding shoe, 36
  tilting shoe, 36

saber saw (*cont.*)
  uses for, 34-35
  variable speed, 39
safety precautions (*see also* under individual
    tools), 4, 5-11, 13, 94
sander, 2, 65-77, 123, 213
  abrasive papers for, 69, 71-73, 76
  auxiliary handle, 70-71
  description of, 66-71
  dust collector, 74
  maintenance of, 77
  operation of, 69, 74-75
  safety precautions for, 71
  selection of, 68-70, 71, 72-73
  types of, 66-70
  uses for, 65, 66, 75
saws, *see* band saw; chain saw; circular saw;
    radial arm saw; saber saw; scroll saw;
    table saw
  basic cuts of, 13-15
scroll (jig) saw, 163-171
  blades for, 163-164, 165, 167-168, 169-171
  cost of, 165
  description of, 164-167
  operation of, 169-171
  safety precautions for, 163
  sanding attachment, 168, 169
  selection of, 165-167
  sizes of, 165-167
  uses for, 163-164
soldering iron, 78-89
  cost of, 78
  electrical power needed for, 79-84
  equipment and materials for, 84-88
    desoldering tool, 86, 87
    flux, 84, 85
    solder, 84, 85
    soldering-aid tool, 86
    solder wick, 86

soldering iron (*cont.*)
  tips, 84, 86
  maintenance of, 89
  operation of, 88-89
  safety precautions for, 86-88
  selection of, 80-84
  types of, 79-84, 85
  uses for, 78-79
straight-line sander, *see* sander

table saw, 35, 51, 148-162
  accessories for, 154, 155-157
    base stand, 154
    dado set, 155, 156
    molding cutter, 156, 157
    table extension, 157
  anti-kickback device, 153
  blade guard, 150, 153
  blades for, 155
  cost of, 149, 152, 153
  description of, 149-153
  maintenance of, 153, 161-162
  miter gauge, 151, 154, 155, 160
  operation of, 153-155, 157-161
  rip fence, 151
  safety precautions for, 150, 153, 158, 161
  selection of, 152-153, 155
  splitter, 150
  uses for, 148, 149, 152, 155
transformerless gun, *see* soldering iron
tree cutting, 181, 185, 187-189
twist drills, 21-22, 24

welder, 221-223
  arc, 221, 222, 223
  gas torch, 222, 223
  operation of, 222
  safety precautions for, 223